HIDDEN TREASURES

SOUTHAMPTON

Edited by Claire Tupholme

First published in Great Britain in 2002 by
YOUNG WRITERS
Remus House,
Coltsfoot Drive,
Peterborough, PE2 9JX
Telephone (01733) 890066

HB ISBN 0 75433 952 1
SB ISBN 0 75433 953 X

FOREWORD

This year, the Young Writers' Hidden Treasures competition proudly presents a showcase of the best poetic talent from over 72,000 up-and-coming writers nationwide.

Young Writers was established in 1991 and we are still successful, even in today's technologically-led world, in promoting and encouraging the reading and writing of poetry.

The thought, effort, imagination and hard work put into each poem impressed us all, and once again, the task of selecting poems was a difficult one, but nevertheless, an enjoyable experience.

We hope you are as pleased as we are with the final selection and that you and your family continue to be entertained with *Hidden Treasures Southampton* for many years to come.

CONTENTS

Blackfield Junior School

Lucy Wainwright	66
Charlotte Pilcher	67
Teri Thomas	68
Hollie Jones	68
Claire Todd	69
Stephanie Hughes	70
Melissa Bainbridge	70
Alex Williams	71
Lee Hutchings	72
Vicki Wilkinson	72
Leanne Cox	73
James Scaum	74
Jessica Davis	74
Decca Brooks	75
Daniel Tonkin	75
Beckie Noon	76
Laura Delaney	77
Gemma Skeggs	78
Joanne Hayward	78
Chrissie Morris	79
Hannah Poole	80
Melissa Hawkins	81
Samantha Ball	82
Kayleigh Taylor	82
Matthew Sait	83
Sarah Kate Jones	84
Jade Hawkins	84
Laura Moody	85
Zoe Hanley	85
Eliot Tibbit	86
Katy Bird	86
Hazel Katie Pugh	87
Kerry Allen	87

Foundry Lane Primary School

Tiffany Heasman	88
Rachel Vear	88
Jennifer Platt	89

Townhill Junior School

The Poems

HIDDEN TREASURES

I often find things are missing, they seem to disappear,
Then a few years later hidden treasures do appear.

I often find the hidden things appear in odd places,
I find many of these, there's been millions of cases.

I often have hidden treasures in my head,
I forget those treasures during school and remember them in bed.

I've dreamt of finding hidden treasures pirates once did own,
But I woke up not on an island, but in bed at home.

I've heard diving people finding treasure in a wreck,
I would love to have a go myself but my feet won't leave the deck.

I once found some hidden treasure by a shop's till,
Only a few pence, definitely not enough to pay the bill.

It's something wonderful whether it's others or mine,
Treasure is something to be treasured through time.

Rachael Smallwood (10)
Blackfield Junior School

HIDDEN TREASURE

He is funny
Have you guessed it's not a bunny

He helps me in class
He runs like the wind on grass

His age is eight
He is my best mate

It's a friend.

Danny Cox (9)
Blackfield Junior School

HIDDEN TREASURE

Hidden treasure under the sea,
Hiding where it shouldn't be.

Hidden under coral,
Hidden under sand,
Hidden under the water,
Or even under land.

There by accident,
There by deed,
Among the fishes,
Covered in weed.

In an old wooden wreck,
In an old wooden chest,
Jewels, silver rings,
With a gold royal crest.

Claire Wilkinson (11)
Blackfield Junior School

HIDDEN TREASURE

The pirates landed on Treasure Island
It was full of palm trees and golden sand
'Now where's that treasure?' one of them said
'We're so tired we could go to bed'
Dig, dig, dig went the spade
The pirates were so hot they needed some shade
Sweat pouring off their skin too bad
Hot work all day makes them so mad
'Aah!' shouted the captain, 'I've found some treasure'
That night they had a party for their great pleasure.

Sarah Muston (8)
Blackfield Junior School

HIDDEN TREASURES

My hidden treasure is a golden box
Nobody knows where it is
It is where I keep my smelly socks
And it really is a big quiz
Oh no, where has it gone?
Where's my golden box?
It must have been abducted by King Kong
It's not with my smelly socks
I ran downstairs and looked on the mantelpiece
Oh no, what have I done?
Phew, it was next to the China geese
After all, it hasn't been abducted by King Kong
Just by my mum.

Charlotte Press (9)
Blackfield Junior School

HIDDEN TREASURES

I can't imagine being a mermaid
With long, blonde golden hair
I can't imagine being a mermaid
Breathing underwater, not coming up for air
I can't imagine being a mermaid
Living with all that silver and gold
I can't imagine being a mermaid
I would probably never grow old
I can't imagine being a mermaid
Having all these fish as friends
I can't imagine being a mermaid
Where my friendship never ends.

Naomi Harvey (11)
Blackfield Junior School

HIDDEN TREASURES

As I began to dig down
I couldn't help but frown
How far away from me
Could this treasure be?
My teacher told me it was hidden
But not in a place forbidden
So where is this treasure
That's going to bring me pleasure
The only clue she gave me
Was look inside and you will see
I try to imagine what I can find
And what it could be behind
Suddenly it all becomes clear
This special treasure is very near
Deep inside my heart
This is a very special part
You do not need to dig or look above
I now realise the hidden treasure is love.

Bethany Scourfield (9)
Blackfield Junior School

HIDDEN TREASURES

As I strolled across the golden sands
The sun in my face
The wind in my hair
I was so happy just being there.

The sun shines so bright, it's so hard to see
But what's that shining up at me?
I kneel in the sand, so I can see
What is hiding down there from me.

A golden crown with rubies like wine
And emeralds so green like I've never seen
The pleasure I feel I can't explain
Excitement running through my veins.

I retrieve my crown from amongst the sand
I stroll slowly back across the sand
But this time with my hidden treasure.

Kirsty West (11)
Blackfield Junior School

HIDDEN TREASURE

There is not a treasure in my mind,
Well not that I could find.
Unless there is one,
That is kept with my mum.
It isn't treasure from the sea,
And it is not kept with me.
I wonder where else it could be.
It might be a toy,
It might well be a bunny,
Or something else quite funny.
50-50, phone a friend, who would know the answer?
Searching high, searching low,
I think the answer has to be 'No!'
It might be lots of money,
Or jars and jars of honey.
My mum said, 'I'll have honey coming out of my ears,
That would surely give me tears.'
I wish I could find
The treasure in my mind.

Marie Atkinson (8)
Blackfield Junior School

HIDDEN TREASURES

I went to the sandy seaside,
Where it had soft sand and a smooth tide.
I went for a short walk,
While my parents had a long talk.
On my way to get an ice cream,
Out of the corner of my eye I had seen,
A glinting shell half buried near the sea, shining like gold.
I ran over to it and only just caught it,
But running down my legs was water freezing cold,
This shell was so wonderful,
So lovely and beautiful,
It was my hidden treasure!

Emily Matthews (10)
Blackfield Junior School

THE JUNGLE'S TREASURE

Fly in the sky like an eagle
Hop down the street like a kangaroo
Throwing spikes is illegal
Is it really true?

Under the sea is some treasure
With some sharks to guard
Maybe it's hard to measure
Maybe it's a fish's backyard.

When we bring the treasure back up
The treasure is really gone.

Nicole Cook (9)
Blackfield Junior School

HIDDEN TREASURES

The sun was getting hot,
The map was very confusing,
I was very bored,
The sand was hot,
My mates were staggering behind me,
We thought we were lost,
We are halfway, thank God for that!
A girl was injured, oh no!
Someone stayed with her,
We carried on going,
Hooray, we're here
We quickly dug a hole
Yes! We found the hidden treasure.

Gemma Johnstone (9)
Blackfield Junior School

HIDDEN TREASURE

My treasure is when a child is in bed,
When the stars and the moon glisten like candles.
It is like the thin line between life and death,
It is the spark that lights the flair of your imagination.
The kick that sends your thoughts running wild,
It can be as gentle as a summer breeze
And yet it could kill you.
My hidden treasure is guessing and finding out . . .

Your destiny.

Craig Diffey (11)
Blackfield Junior School

HIDDEN TREASURE

I have something that I treasure
I take it everywhere
It gives me so much pleasure
It's my teddy bear!

My bear has the biggest smile
And a beautiful orange mane
He sits on the top of the pile
And Elvis is his name.

Elvis and I enjoy playing together
Especially hide and seek
He often is my hidden treasure
And we play it every week.

Michelle Tanner (8)
Blackfield Junior School

HIDDEN TREASURES

One day I went to the Natural History Museum
To see lots of hidden treasure
And I had lots of pleasure
The first thing I saw
Was the diplodocus dinosaur.
The petrified wood really made me surprised
At the top and bottom of my eyes
My dad was as scared as could be
At the reptiles he could see
The gems were as big as M&Ms
And shiny as can be
And I wish they were all for me.

Joseph Hanley (7)
Blackfield Junior School

HIDDEN TREASURE

Go diving for treasure
And if you find it
You will be in pleasure.

Now get your goggles and aqualung on
Get to that rock and take your plunge.

Now what is that sparkling in the sea at night
I think it's the treasure
No, it's only a white bait in fright.

But what is it frightened of
Maybe it's a bluresure fish
I think I should go back to the surface
Oh look, there's the bluresure fish
No wait, it's the treasure.

David Down (11)
Blackfield Junior School

HIDDEN TREASURE

Down at the beach there is an old cave,
It is so old that it is falling down.
Inside though it's dark,
There is a box made of bark and wood.
It has a huge padlock made of brass.
Deeper down in the cave is a huge key
Made of brass for the clasp.
I went down there one day and opened the box.
Inside I found some *hidden treasure!*

Oliver Hayward (10)
Blackfield Junior School

HIDDEN TREASURES

One late afternoon
There was a baboon
Her name was Lin
And she had a great grin!

She sits in the trees
Made comfortable by leaves
She saw the sun
Looking like a currant bun.

There was not much food
And this put her in a mood
Spying out of one eye
She thought she would die!

At the top of the tree
She did see
A branch full of fruit
The smile on her face made her look cute!

You would never have known
That hidden in her home
Was a branch full of treasure
To give her some pleasure!

Hannah Cole (8)
Blackfield Junior School

HIDDEN TREASURE

There are many forms of treasure
Gold and silver give people pleasure
Many people like lots of things
Necklaces, bracelets and diamond rings

But the best hidden treasure
For me is out there
It's my life and being able
To breathe fresh air.

Alice Cole (9)
Blackfield Junior School

HIDDEN TREASURE

Down in the deep blue sea
Is where they sent me.
I was meant to find the treasure
But came upon some heather.

Down in the deep blue sea
Is where they sent me.
I have to dive . . .
Oh, my name is *Clive.*

Down in the deep blue sea
Is where they sent me.
I saw some lovely fish
I wish they were on my dinner dish.

Down in the deep blue sea
Is where they sent me.
I came upon a stone
Upon it was a phone.

Down in the deep blue sea
Is where they sent me.
My air ran out, I couldn't get out
So I stayed in the deep blue sea.

Thomas Sheppard (8)
Blackfield Junior School

LIFE IS A HIDDEN TREASURE

Life is a hidden treasure,
Which is locked up in the heart.
It will bring you great pleasure,
If you dig down and are smart.

It's a gift which is given to you,
Only once in your life.
So remember never to be blue,
And live without strife.

You can't unlock it with a key,
Don't waste it, trust me.
Just remember live your life with glee,
Life is great you will see.

You can make many choices day by day,
That will change the way you live.
Enjoy this come what may,
Open your heart and learn to live.

Craig Scourfield (11)
Blackfield Junior School

HIDDEN TREASURE

Walking through the shadowy cave,
I look around for treasure.
Beneath my feet there might be a crawly crab,
And you never know when you're going to find one.

I dive down into the water,
Surrounded by fish and coral.
All you can hear is water
Rushing by your ear.

I haven't found any treasure,
But I've found some shells instead.
The beauty of the sea is treasure in itself,
The multicoloured fish are the treasure of the sea.

Kelly Prewitt (9)
Blackfield Junior School

HIDDEN TREASURE

As I walked around the island
I was thinking about the Highlands
In the sand my feet were sinking.

The island had some palm trees
And in the breeze they were blowing
The sea looked like it was going to overflow.

I saw some birds high in the sky
And over my head
They flew on by.

I saw a boat
Which seemed to just float
And the boat was big.

I looked through the bushes
And there before my eyes
I saw a small box.

Inside the box I had found the hidden treasure
I saw some coins
Which glittered in the sun.

Charlotte Longworth (8)
Blackfield Junior School

HIDDEN TREASURES

There are hidden treasures under the sea,
Waiting for you and me.
You'll be surprised when you see what's inside,
It might be gold or diamonds.
The treasure chest won't open,
Unless you find the key.
The key is behind something green,
It could be behind coral or seaweed,
Just go down there and see.
It's right behind the treasure chest,
Don't go down there at night.
Because the fish will give you a *fright.*
If you go down there in the day light,
You'll get a big *delight!*
Seeing all the beautiful colours,
Of the bright coloured fish.
I hope you like the hidden treasures,
At the bottom of the sea.
Just follow my advice,
And I hope you find the key.
So good luck,
Searching for the treasure and key!

Emily Poole (8)
Blackfield Junior School

HIDDEN TREASURE

As I turn around I stop and stare
will the treasure be in there?
As I walk in the dark cave
someone speaks my name, Dave.

'The treasure is in the ditch,'
I say to myself I'm going to be rich.
When I get the red ring
I'll be as rich as the king.

Billy Morton (9)
Blackfield Junior School

HIDDEN TREASURES

Hidden treasure, where can you be?
Here I am below the sea.
The light above is fading fast,
I must move quick while it lasts.

Deeper, deeper, deeper I go,
I hope I can find the treasure below.
I see a glimmer, is this it?
But oh no, it's just a fish.

It is very dark below the sea,
I wish my mum was here with me.
Where, oh where can it be?
I wish it could come to me.

I've had enough I'm going back,
I knew this dream would not last.
But when I'm back in bed tonight,
I'll shut my eyes really tight.

I hope my dream will come to me,
When I dive under the sea.
I know I'll find the rainbow's end,
Then the pot of gold I can spend.

Jade Edginton (10)
Blackfield Junior School

TREASURE!

Treasure is special
Treasure is gold
Treasure is found
Treasure is sold.

Sometimes it is silver
Sometimes it is pearls
Sometimes it is bronze
Or my mum's chocolate swirls.

It sparkles like the stars
It sparkles like the sea
It sparkles like the sun
Treasure is special to me.

Stephanie Smallwood (8)
Blackfield Junior School

HIDDEN TREASURE

It stands tall and proud like a huge mountain covered in crisp,
clean snow.
I stare at it in amazement wondering if I will ever be able to beat it.
The colours of the layers change as I come down to the bottom.
I know that at the very base of this challenging ice mountain
is the treasure I have been looking for.
My digging equipment is strong and shiny and I prepare to go in.
After what seemed like a lifetime of digging,
the climax of my adventure suddenly arrived.
The sparkling jewels at the bottom of my ice cream sundae
shimmered in the sunlight.
With one last dig my mouth was full of pleasure
I have conquered my ice cream sundae and found the hidden treasure.

Daryl Price (8)
Blackfield Junior School

HIDDEN TREASURE

Hidden deep underground in a damp dark cave,
Impossible to be seen from above
Deeper than the dinosaur bones
Damper than a soaking flannel
Everybody wants the treasure
Nobody can find it.

Today more people go in search of the treasure
Ready to dig up bones and fossils
Even though they will not find the treasure
A hundred people go off in search
Still looking after centuries, it is still not found
Under 1000 tons of dirt lies the treasure
Ready to dig for the treasure my son goes
Everyone fails to find it
So nobody can find it and nobody will find my hidden treasure.

Jack Shepherd (11)
Blackfield Junior School

HIDDEN TREASURES

Cats and dogs in the street,
Rats and mice creep and creep.
Rabbit and fox run and chase
A prickly hedgehog in a safer place.

A busy bee buzzing around,
Making a peculiar sort of sound.
A mole in a hole with his dark, dark fur
And a cat comes along with a sly, slick purr.
All of these animals are life's little treasures
And each of them brings us little pleasures.

Sophia Britton (7)
Blackfield Junior School

DIVING FOR TREASURES

Deeper and deeper
In I go
Looking for treasures
Under the sea
Digging in the seabed
On the way I go
I can see lots of creatures
Like a
Skate fish
And there are sea creatures
And there is
The treasures
And then you
Can dig it out
Then swim
Away with it.

Mark Fleat (10)
Blackfield Junior School

HIDDEN TREASURES

I have a memory that no one else can see
It is very special to me
It is the day I got my brown wooden playhouse
It was fun, exciting and such a surprise
I could not believe my eyes
All my friends came to play
Until it was the end of the day
That is my memory in my head
And it won't go until I'm dead.

Lucie McGonagle (8)
Blackfield Junior School

THE HIDDEN TREASURE

Sailing in my cardboard ship across the front room floor,
Tea towel bandanna on my head slicing up sea monsters, dead.
Slowly I approach sirens upon the kitchen table,
One of them is Gertrude and the other one is Mabel.
'Ahoy there girls, where is my treasure? Tell me now
and continue your pleasure.
If you don't I'll stab you dead and use you both as a figure head!'
'Back off sailor, or we'll start singing and that'll start
your ears a-ringing!'
'Oh please be nice to me,' I said, 'because it's nearly time for bed!'
The mermaids looked down at me from afar,
'Your treasure is up there in the cookie jar!'
I carefully climbed upon the kitchen table,
Almost stepping on Gertie and Mabel.
Reaching high to the top shelf, trying to achieve my tummy's wealth.
All at once the shelf fell down, cookie jar and all,
My treasure lost and crumbled out into the hall,
Mum rushed in and gave a shout,
'All you three children, please *get out!*'

Joshua March (10)
Blackfield Junior School

HIDDEN TREASURE

Dive, dive, dive,
You will have to survive.
We're diving for lost treasure.

We would like to find gold,
So we'll have to be bold,
But to find it will be a pleasure.

Thomas Holmes (7)
Blackfield Junior School

THE HIDDEN TREASURE

Down the stairs and in the kitchen,
There lies some hidden treasure,
Mum thinks that she has hidden them
But I sneak them at my leisure.

When we are good and well behaved
She treats us to a few
Even though I know I shouldn't
I still try to sneak more than two.

I hope that she never finds out
When there are some missing
Wish I had my own small stash
But here's wishing.

If you haven't guessed by now
What are the treats?
The hidden treasure is of course
Lovely, lovely sweets.

Christopher White (11)
Blackfield Junior School

HIDDEN TREASURES

Hidden treasures are hard to find,
Every one a different kind.
Jewellery, gifts and shiny gold,
Precious gifts I want to hold.

Treasure is not always what it seems,
It maybe to someone a simple sunbeam.
We all possess them, they're not always seen,
We have to look and we'd have to be keen.

We all have something special to keep,
Hidden well and hidden deep.
There maybe treasures inside me and you,
If you look hard you'll find one too.

Catherine Moody (9)
Blackfield Junior School

MY HIDDEN TREASURES

I was exploring the garden in the autumn sunshine
What could I find?
The leaves were turning red, yellow and brown
Suddenly I saw movement
Little caterpillars, green with yellow stripes
I looked for them every day
As it got colder, they hid in dead leaves.

When spring arrived I discovered chrysalises
Brown and dull, they looked dead, hidden in leaves
I wonder what they will become?
Will they be white, yellow, green or some other colour?
I keep watch day by day
And then suddenly something flutters into the air
I watch with baited breath
It flies towards me
Settles on my hand and spreads its wings
As the light catches them
They sparkle like sapphires
Deep, deep blue
As beautiful as any precious stone
My own special treasure, no longer hidden
A rare Adonis blue butterfly.

Chantelle Hayne-Bell (11)
Blackfield Junior School

HIDDEN TREASURES

'Surely you can do some maths?'
My mother said to me.
'No, no, no, I can't do it,
I prefer history.'
'But what about plus, subtract, divide?'
She said as she sipped her coffee.
'No I can't, it's way too hard,
I can't do maths for toffee!'
In only a week the test arrived,
The hardest maths of all.
'I won't make it,' I told my friends,
'I won't make it at all.'
And when it came I was really scared,
My face was dripping with sweat,
I worried when it came to me,
About the questions I'd be set.
But it was easy, simple, pimps,
I whizzed through with brilliant speed,
And when I looked at the scoreboard,
I was in the lead!
'I can do maths!' I told myself,
'That was kind of fun.'
I got better marks than anyone,
Wait till I tell my mum!

Steven Christian Allen (10)
Blackfield Junior School

MY BABY BROTHER

My baby brother is a little treasure
To our house he's full of joy and pleasure
He maybe cute, he maybe small
But for a baby he's really cool

He's got no teeth, he's got no hair
But when he's older, girls beware!
He sucks his dummy and plays with toys
But I am glad my mum had a baby boy.

Holly Kinggett (8)
Blackfield Junior School

HIDDEN TREASURE

I went on holiday to the sea,
My mother, father and sister too.
We went to stay at an old cottage,
My bedroom had a lovely view.

Across the road there was a beach,
Which was lovely and pretty too.
My sister and I went to play,
And that is where it is nice and cool.

We played around the windy beach,
The seagulls liked to scream
But it started to rain hard,
So it wasn't good to have ice cream.

It was still brightly sunny,
But it was still raining anyway.
Then we saw a rainbow's end . . .
It wasn't far away.

We heard stories of pots of gold,
Hidden at the end of rainbows.
Maybe we'll find some hidden treasure,
When we come back tomorrow.

Harry Dugdale (10)
Blackfield Junior School

HIDDEN TREASURES

I was looking into a forest of seaweed
Feathery green, swishing in the water
At the bottom were grey gravel stones
Some tiny castles and pots on a quarter.

Bubbles came swishing from the pump
Bursting on the surface
The darkness was as thick as fog
Making it seem a weird place.

I saw a sudden splash of colour
I blinked and looked again
A flash of gold, a dash of silver
Colours like a rainbow in the rain.

Fish came swimming out of the weeds
Gold and silver just like treasure
Orange, red, purple and blue
All of them were mine forever and ever.

Christopher Chester-Sterne (8)
Blackfield Junior School

THE WAKING FOREST

As the sun rises and the moon sinks
The fieldmice sleep, the owl blinks.
The birds are waking, each in its nest,
The fox slinks wearily back to rest.

The trees dance in the early light
As the birds sing goodbye to the night.
The deer come shyly out of shade
To the open land the kestrels raid.

Rabbits snatch the last patch of grass,
Watching the squirrels as they pass.
From the bank the otter dives,
Like a furry torpedo ending lives.

Christopher Barton (10)
Blackfield Junior School

HIDDEN TREASURE!

Only after the last tree has been cut down,
Only after the last river has been poisoned,
Only after the last fish has been caught,
Only then will you find out that money cannot be eaten.

Only after the last mighty war has been won,
Only after the last goodies have won.
Only after the last baddies have gone far away,
Only then we can find the hidden treasure.

Only after you've been deep in the sea,
Only after you've been deep in the dark forest,
Only after you've been deep in the jungle,
Only then you can dig a hole for the treasure.

Only after you've found the hidden treasure,
Only after you've opened the treasure box,
Only after you've made sure it's real treasure,
Only after you go to the Lord.

Only after you've found the Lord,
Only after you've reached the Lord,
Only after he's seen the treasure
Only then you can be free.

Abigail Sara Moffatt (10)
Blackfield Junior School

HIDDEN TREASURES

She was worried
She was sad
But her mum was really glad
Her mum was getting bigger and bigger.

Would it be a girl?
Would it be a boy?
Either one would it bring joy?
Her mum said it was not a toy.

If it was a boy it should be called Roy,
If it was a girl it should be called Pearl.
She wasn't sure what it would be useful for,
Her mum said wait and see, it will be fun for you and me.

When she was born it was a girl,
She certainly turned out to be a pearl.
Her mum always said it would bring pleasure,
She guessed it was a hidden treasure.

Gemma Saxby (11)
Blackfield Junior School

HIDDEN TREASURE

What is this, a shiny box?
I know, it's not a sly fox
Wait, I think it's hidden treasure
I think it was supposed to be hidden there forever
The gold was so shiny bright
I had to fight to get to the light
It was not pants or socks
My goodness, look at those golden rocks!

Gracie Wainwright (8)
Blackfield Junior School

HIDDEN TREASURE

I rowed my dinghy very far,
to a small beach covered in tar.

I had a map to hidden treasure,
which I knew would give me pleasure.

I trudged on through the sand,
until I saw a mine which was grand.

In the mine I saw a chest,
it was older than the rest.

It was full of silver and gold,
which was very old.

I am now very happy,
no longer grumpy, sad or snappy.

Shane A Trim (8)
Blackfield Junior School

TREASURES OF THE DEEP

On a bright, sunny day
I bravely made my way
To the waters deep and cold
Hoping to find the treasures of gold
Lying deep in the sea, in the wreck of a ship
With my diving suit on, into the waters I slip
There the old sunken ship lies, I hope the treasure is inside
By the mast, I spy the chest lying beside
With all my might I lift the chest to the top
I feel so happy I could pop.

Michael Trim (11)
Blackfield Junior School

HIDDEN TREASURE

I sit and read a pirate book
Tales from the sea of Captain Hook
I sometimes wish I could be
A pirate out in the deep blue sea
For the thought of gold from the stories old
Hidden treasure, where it is I won't be told.

In my dream there's gold and gems
Before I come back home again
Because on the other side of my bedroom door
There is the greatest treasure of all
My mum!

Callum Smyth (9)
Blackfield Junior School

HIDDEN TREASURES

My treasures aren't gold, silver or diamonds
They are cousins, grandparents, aunts and uncles
They make me feel part of the family
When we are all together, I get really excited
And very, very cheeky
We all take care of each other
I get looked after by the older ones
And I look after the younger ones
It makes me feel important
Like I should keep them safe
Some people don't feel like that about their families
My family are my hidden treasures.

Freddie Bools (8)
Blackfield Junior School

HIDDEN TREASURES: SECRETS OF THE DEEP!

Deeper and deeper I go,
Picking up delicacies along the way,
All the treasures you could think of,
But none as great as this . . .

Is what I see a wondrous wreck,
Darkness shadows over its hold,
It could not take the water's edge,
'Twas smashed against the rocks!

That bonny galleon still survives,
On the bottom of the ocean,
Treasures inside are covered with anemones,
But, that does not hide its fate!

I lifted its lid, 'twas barnacle covered,
Treasures of all kinds, gold and silver,
Any greedy man would take all its worth,
But, never live to tell the tale!

If it's stolen shalt take on a curse,
A curse of much unkindness,
A sinister death is waiting on offer,
To anyone who has the urge to steal it!

Out I swam, for the cold struck me fast,
Past the colourful fish illuminating in the light,
I did not gasp for they would flee,
Never to be seen again!

Up and up till I reached the surface,
I swam, from the mysteries I'd left behind,
The wreck is left to itself,
For future generations to come!

Rachael Oke (11)
Blackfield Junior School

HIDDEN TREASURE

The deep blue sea hid a secret to tell
Out from the fog sailed a pirate's ship
From the crow's nest came a loud yell
'Land ahoy!' he shouted, with a slap of his hip

Were the stories true or just folklore?
They quickly loaded their shovel and picks
As they had done many times before
Or was the island up to its mysterious tricks?

Once they stepped on to the sandy beach
They decided to make camp for the night
Was the hidden treasure within their reach?
The captain's plan so far was right.

A good night's sleep, then up bright and early
They all set off with the treasure map
The captain's crew were all big and burly
Would they be heading towards a trap?

Through the jungle, then over the hill
As the sun shone brightly down
Cautiously they trekked, pacing, until
They stopped suddenly and all wore a frown.

Was this the treasure spot? They all called, 'It's mine!'
And started to dig. Soon they had a massive great ditch
The treasure chest they had found was fine
They had finally become rich!

Samuel Williams (11)
Blackfield Junior School

THE HIDDEN TREASURE

When I got home from school I went to bed,
Resting my poor, tired, sleepy head,
Then later on I heard a bang, so I picked up my bear
And went down the stair.
I saw lots of water all over the floor,
Someone had opened the washing machine door,
I swam through the water to get to the door,
So the water couldn't get out anymore!
By now the washing machine was on spin,
Oh no, look out, I'm being sucked in!
The next thing I knew I was crying, boo hoo,
The washing was spinning but with me in too!
Sucked up the pipe and gushed down the drain,
Dirty washing water mixed up with the rain,
I found myself spurted out into the sea,
I met this fish and he gave me a key.
'This key will open the ship's ancient lock,
The ship over there by the enormous rock.'
We swam over to the door, then had a rest,
Before we looked for the treasure chest.
We had to go to the seventh floor,
After we'd opened the right door.
We found the treasure chest on the floor,
The fish and I opened the chest lid as a pair,
The treasure inside was a new baby bear.
I cuddled it tight all through the night,
So I didn't have another fright.

Bradley March (9)
Blackfield Junior School

HIDDEN TREASURE

Where may it be?
How is it found?
It is not for me to see.
It could be as high as the mountains,
Or maybe as low as the ground.

How can I find it?
Is it close maybe far?
Will I find all of it, or just a tiny bit?
What shape does it take?
A sphere, oblong or even a bar.

Is it big,
Or small?
Could it be as thin as a twig.
Or as thick as a building?
Would it be boring or would it be cool?

Without me realising,
Here it is in me,
There was no way of noticing.
But I have found it now,
There's no need to look, it was always with me.

Sharni Carr (10)
Blackfield Junior School

NATURE'S HIDDEN TREASURES

Dewdrops like diamonds shine everywhere,
Ruby red poppies nod in the air
Grass, green as emeralds,
A sapphire blue sky
A big golden sun,
Silver clouds drifting by.

Pearly white roses smell sweet as can be,
Sunflowers like crowns, everywhere you can see,
These are my treasures,
My heart and my soul,
More precious than jewels,
They make me feel whole.

Lydia Townsend (9)
Blackfield Junior School

HIDDEN TREASURES

My friend and I set out to sea,
The two of us, just her and me.
We paddled with our toes in the sand,
Then suddenly she took my hand.

We jumped and dived right through the tide,
But with me she stayed by my side.
But as we slipped through seaweed and murk,
We saw caves and rocks where fishes lurk.

Pearls a-dazzle, seaweed drift,
But what came next was the biggest gift.
My friend saw I wasn't OK,
My body felt weak and there I lay.

She glided down with all her might,
I couldn't breathe, my lungs were tight.
As we reached the surface I then found,
I didn't need a treasure mound.

The treasure wasn't deep down in the sea,
The treasure was right here . . . with me.

Nicola Humphriss (11)
Blackfield Junior School

HIDDEN TREASURES

H idden treasures are people to me,
I love my family like jewels,
D addy is really, really special,
D affodils are as golden as the sun.
E very girl and boy has loving parents,
N ever be unkind to anyone.

T ulips are a colourful treasure
R oses are red like rubies
E merald is my birth stone,
A pples are treasures off a tree,
S ausages sizzle in a pan,
U sually treasures are wherever you look,
R eally special people are my family,
E xtra treasure is hidden in the sea,
S leep tight with all of your treasures.

Charlotte Willbourne (8)
Blackfield Junior School

THE WHALE

I'm diving in the sea,
I wonder what I'll see.
I met a whale, he spoke to me,
He said his goodbyes and followed me.
Faster I swam until *yummy!*
He gobbled me up.
Then I wondered who or what was the hidden treasure
Maybe me
Or maybe I'm yet to know.

Emily Burden (11)
Blackfield Junior School

34

HIDDEN TREASURES

I know
Something lies beneath the deepest depths of the deep sea,
Ascending through the misty moon-blue water.
Waiting in hunger
With its rumbling stomach gurgling vigorously!
I read on page after page.
Hours tick by on the clock on the wall.
Suddenly I realise the truth.

The monster's going to come up and chew me till I'm dead.
I snap my book shut!
Pictures play on my mind for hours like they do on Christmas Eve.
There's nothing better than a good book!

Rhiannon Hardie (10)
Blackfield Junior School

HIDDEN TREASURE

My family gives me warmth and care
that no one else can share.

It shows me love and understanding
even when we're not there.

My family you see are the best hidden treasure
there can be.

You can keep your gold, jewels and money
Just let me have my dad and mummy, and a nice full tummy.

This is you see because they are the best hidden treasure
there can be, especially to me.

Marsha Davage (8)
Blackfield Junior School

HIDDEN TREASURE

H is for hiding the treasure
I n the salty blue sea
D is for diving
D iving is like surviving
E ven the duck can swim and dive
N elly the elephant can survive

T reasure in the salty water
R ings are nice, they touch you on the knee
E is for eastern treasure glowing
A is for angel that keep it safe
S is for seaweed that is green
U is for under the water
R is for river that is going to the sea
E is for easy, the treasure has been found.

Lauren Sharpe (7)
Blackfield Junior School

HIDDEN TREASURES

Far, far away on a secret island
In the middle of the deep blue sea
There lived a clever talking parrot
He was as orange as a carrot
A long time ago after the biggest tidal wave
The parrot found a spooky cave
Out of the corner of his eye a treasure chest he did spy
He pecked it open and found one million pounds
He carried the pounds one by one
To England to have some fun.

Nicholas Shrive (7)
Blackfield Junior School

HIDDEN TREASURE

Hidden in boxes
Where the foxes
Don't dare go
Where the grass can't grow

Where the boxes
Lay is unknown
That pirates used to own
Which have lost a shin bone

I am looking here and there
I am looking everywhere
Is it here, is it there?
I can't find it anywhere

I searched high and low
Until at last
I found the box of brass.

Billy Mainwaring (11)
Blackfield Junior School

HIDDEN TREASURE

Down at the bottom of the sea
There is a big spotty octopus waiting for me
At the end of his eight legs
Lay a nasty old pot
Filled with treasure up to the top
It was pink and green
And can only be seen
By a very clever girl like me.

Sarah Jones (8)
Blackfield Junior School

HIDDEN TREASURE

Down I go
Till the water turns cold
And the air is blue
At last, the knight so bold
Has found his damsel in distress

He uncovers the mess
And sees his life of fun
Cos he needs now nothing
From what he has done
Now all his life is shattered

His house is clattered
From the robbers
To the snatchers

And he is down again
At the sea
The water now bitterly cold
Again down he goes
With everything he has not sold

Now the damsel is back home
Free to someone else
Now the knight is back
With his ordinary life
The treasure he always had.

Tom Beardmore (11)
Blackfield Junior School

HIDDEN TREASURES

In a field long ago,
I found hidden treasure with my hoe!
I took my find to those who know,
Who told me this was treasure trove.

I cashed it in and to my delight,
I could afford a motorbike!
With the change I bought a metal detector,
And started searching another sector!

Phillip Trim (9)
Blackfield Junior School

HIDDEN TREASURES

Down below on the seabed,
There lies a treasure chest,
It lies there
For days and days,
For someone to end its rest.
Fish swim by,
Happy as can be,
But they do not know
What that thing could be.

Divers look
In the most difficult places,
But they do not know
That it is in one of the easiest spaces,
They look and look,
For days and days,
But in those days
They do not
Find anything
At all.

Down below on the seabed
There lies a treasure chest.

Robyn Young (11)
Blackfield Junior School

HIDDEN TREASURE

Why are waves so peaceful,
Yet sometimes so mad,
Is it something I've done,
That made them sad.

What did I do?
Was it stupid or selfish?
Did I pollute the sea?
It must have been bad,
Believe me.

Is it like a angry tiger,
That has not been fed,
And if you go too far out
You may end up dead.

But if you go down
Just to the sea's bed
On the sunken Armada
The treasure to be found
We search even harder.

We have not found
The millionaire ship
Lumps and bars of solid gold
That have been left in the freezing cold.

Mark Shea (11)
Blackfield Junior School

HIDDEN TREASURE

We've come to the island to look for the treasure
And I know if we find some, it will give me great pleasure.
Trees in front, sand on the beach,
A hill in the distance that looks out of reach.

Treasure is found and treasure is sold,
Treasure is silver and lots of gold.
Diamonds and pearls, coins of gold,
You'll be rich until you're old.

Ashleigh Gibbs (9)
Blackfield Junior School

HIDDEN TREASURES

The current swiftly pushed me against a rock,
An oyster's mouth opened wide
Then it revealed a pearl inside,
I gave it a knock,
It suddenly closed like a rock.

None of this has satisfied me yet,
None of this has satisfied me
About the deep blue sea,
Actually . . . I bet
That I've not seen a thousandth of the sea just yet

None of this has satisfied me anyhow
None of this has satisfied me
About the great blue sea
Then just now
I saw a ships bow

Now this has satisfied me
Oh yes, it is, it certainly is
Some ships of the Spanish Armada

Air

No, I need more time
But then thinking I can always come back.

Devon Mayhew (10)
Blackfield Junior School

JUNGLE ADVENTURE

The treasure is in the jungle
To find it is going to be tough
There will be many dangerous animals
And the journey is going to be rough
I feel very scared and excited
I could end up rich, or I could die
It will be a great adventure
I don't know whether to laugh or cry
There will be monkeys, spiders and snakes
I better be on my guard
Because they will all want to hurt me
I can do it, but it will be very hard.

Danielle Knieriem (10)
Blackfield Junior School

DIVING FOR TREASURE

Down, down, down we go,
Against the run of the water's flow,
There was something down there that caught my eye,
On the seabed where someone said it would lie.

I called for help to get it out,
When it was open there was a loud shout,
People fainted, people cheered.
What to do with it was what I feared.

I opened the chest of treasure,
It gave me so much pleasure.

Daniel Fry (11)
Blackfield Junior School

HIDDEN TREASURES - THE BOY'S INNER SOUL

A boy standing on the basketball court
Bounces the ball,
It hits the ground
And hits him in the face.

His friend, seeing he is sad,
Invites him to a game of football,
He agrees and walks onto the pitch,
He takes the position of midfield.

Thinking he is no good,
He kicks the ball,
It sails through the air
And lands in the net.

At last he has found his hidden treasure . . .
. . . football.

Simon Bailey (10)
Blackfield Junior School

HIDDEN TREASURES

One day a little boy and his dad went scuba-diving
'Why are we going scuba-diving?' said Jim
'Because we are going to find hidden treasures,' said Dad
So they set off to find hidden treasures
Halfway down Jim could see a golden chest
'Dad, look a treasure chest,' said Jim
Dad and Jim picked the golden chest up
When they opened the chest they found a golden cup.

Thomas Pothecary (8)
Blackfield Junior School

HIDDEN TREASURES

I am not a pearl,
Nor am I a chest,
I live inside a rock face,
There I always rest.
I have waited many years,
For an avalanche to come,
And bring me crashing down,
There I lie to be discovered for what I am.
Many think of me as boring,
I think though not the same,
I am not what others think,
I am not so very plain.
   I am but the keeper of an extinct, ancient creature,
   On the surface I am plain and light,
   Down below I am . . .
   a trilobite.

Joe Thomas (10)
Blackfield Junior School

HIDDEN TREASURES

Down in the forest lots of prickly chestnuts under a huge tree
All the prickly chestnuts look like prickly hedgehogs
The huge tree looks like she is putting her arms out
I picked up some of the lovely chestnuts and took them home
I took off the shell and grilled them
They popped and *banged,* and soon they were ready to eat
That's my hidden treasure.

Megan Calvert (8)
Blackfield Junior School

HIDDEN TREASURE

The sea is so blue
I need to dive with you
It was so tiny
And it was very, very shiny

It was a very big box
And had loads of padlocks
It was really cold
But the big shiny box was very gold

The box was quite brown
And I was forty metres down
I had to measure
To get the wonderful treasure
And what a lovely pleasure.

Ben Knight (11)
Blackfield Junior School

THE HIDDEN TREASURE

As I walked along the rocky shore with bucket and spade in hand.
On sandy beaches I grabbed my sister's hand,
Though young at heart, clear of mind took us far
I imagined I was a pirate captain sailing the seven seas.
My sister wanted to be a fairy queen, but pirates have no use of these.
I told her she could be my mate, the one in charge of treasure.
'But Andrew, we have no treasure. What treasure would be that?'
'Ah, but look here Sis, in this rocky pool or near the sandy shore,
There are hidden treasures everywhere, just waiting to be explored.'

Andrew Adams (11)
Blackfield Junior School

HIDDEN TREASURE

Treasure is special
Sometimes it's gold or silver
It could be bronze indeed
But normally it's all of these
With some gems probably.

Treasure could be hidden anywhere
Quite often under sea
Where most of it would be
But in actual fact
It could be hidden anywhere.

Treasure doesn't have to be gold or gems
Or anything like that
Treasure could be just love and care
But it doesn't really matter.

Treasure is a kind gift
That's been given to us from God
It isn't money, gold or gems
It's all our love and care.

Colette Marie Hayes (8)
Blackfield Junior School

WINTER'S HIDDEN TREASURES

Winter is rain falling from the sky,
Winter is clouds passing by,
Winter is ice falling from up high,
Winter carries hidden treasures.

Kia Hancock (9)
Blackfield Junior School

HIDDEN TREASURES

In my hand I held a spade,
There underneath me a treasure was laid.
I knew it might take a long time to find,
But I had to let my stress unwind.
Some dug in the ground
While others looked around.
The earth was hard to dig,
So my muscles grew really big.
My hole got wider and wider
And I screamed at the sight of a spider.
But all of a sudden my spade made a sound,
What was this I had found?
Yes! This is where I thought it would be,
I looked inside the hole to see.
Man, I had a big surprise,
Cans of beans were my prize.
So guess what I had for tea instead of Sunday roast
Baked beans piled high on lots of buttery toast!

Mark Stevens (8)
Blackfield Junior School

HIDDEN TREASURE

Up in the attic where nobody goes
Is there treasure? No one knows
If there is and if it you find
Don't you think in your mind
That it is yours?

Stuart Byrne (9)
Blackfield Junior School

HIDDEN TREASURE

Sea calm,
Sea beautiful,
On a mission,
Not for scenery,
Have to find gold,
Rubies, sapphires!
My mouth waters at the thought!

Got to get it!
Got to have it!
I put on my aqualungs
And plunge.
I marvel at the fish,
Seaweed and calmness,
But I must carry on.
I have it in sight!
But I leave it for another day,
As the cold gets to me.

I surface,
Only to see the normal world!

Scott Rollinson (11)
Blackfield Junior School

HIDDEN TREASURE

My treasure is in the forest,
And that's where it stays,
Everyday I visit it,
In a tree trunk where it lays.

No one knows where it's kept,
Not in a bush but in a tree,
None of my friends know where it is,
Only the birds and the bees.

If anybody found it,
I don't know what I would do,
My secret would be out,
And be everyone else's too.

My treasure is a secret,
For only my eyes to see,
My treasure is a secret,
So don't tell anyone please.

Alice Liddon (9)
Blackfield Junior School

HIDDEN TREASURES

I am getting prepared to dive!
Down the deep blue sea,
To find amazing creatures.
But where is the treasure?

Now I'm in the water,
I can see lots of fish,
I have not seen any crabs yet,
But where is the treasure?

I am on the last bit of my journey,
Down beneath the deep blue sea,
Can I see the last minute change
But where is the treasure?

The walls were closing towards me,
As I struggled back to the surface,
As the current pulled me back to the seabed
And I was back to the ordinary world.

Jessica Gregory (10)
Blackfield Junior School

HIDDEN TREASURE

I dive down deep,
To the bottom of the sea
Where I might find jewels,
Or a little golden key.

When I get down there,
I find nothing but seaweed,
But when I turn around,
I see all that I need.

But, oh no!
Oxygen's what I need!

I rush back up to the surface
Where I think,
Will I ever see the treasure again?

Rhiannon Maule (10)
Blackfield Junior School

HIDDEN TREASURES

Diamonds like dew,
On an autumn spider's web.

Rubies like roses,
Pretty in the grass.

Gold like the sun,
On a midsummer's day.

Silver like the moon,
On a midwinter's night.

These are the hidden treasures of nature.

Robin Henderson (10)
Blackfield Junior School

HIDDEN TREASURE

I was a little girl,
I had to move house,
I wanted to take my pearl,
We were out in a flash.

Ten years later,
I went back to that house,
The minute I got to the attic,
I saw a mouse.
But I didn't mind
Because there in the corner,
Was my little pearl.
I picked it up and gave it a twirl.

Rachel Humphriss (9)
Blackfield Junior School

HIDDEN TREASURE

Down and down
And down we go.
It's getting deeper
As we go.

The sea is moving
Round and round.
It's pushing our bodies
Up and down.

We got the treasure
In our hands.
Smiles on our faces
As we head for the sand.

Charlotte Skeggs (9)
Blackfield Junior School

HIDDEN TREASURES

My hidden treasure's at the bottom of the sea
All the little fish are swimming round me
I found my gold at the bottom of the ship
It was like the sea had given me a big tip

My hidden treasure's in the back of the caves
Out of the way of really big waves
In the cave it's dark and gloomy
I can fit my treasure in there because it's roomy

My hidden treasure's under my bed
In a box which is black and red
Something only my eyes can see
It's a personal secret just for me

My hidden treasure's in the bottom of my heart
For no one else to see or feel
Not in a cupboard, not on a shelf
My heart is the hidden treasure I have for myself.

Joshua Liddon (11)
Blackfield Junior School

HIDDEN TREASURE

My best treasure is my Game Boy
It's better than any other toy.
I have lots of games to play on it
But the best game I have is Pokémon.

Game Boy can be tiring
If you play on it too much.
It's just the right size for my pocket
And it doesn't have to be plugged into a socket.

I hide it in my secret box
Which is underneath my socks.
I don't ever want it found
So I keep it safe and sound.

Mathew Tanner (9)
Blackfield Junior School

A WEALTHY QUEST

As I enter the adventurous cave,
There is very fine sand spread across the floor,
Washed up driftwood,
And scuttling bugs enjoying a gnaw.

As mouldy water drips from up above,
Seagulls screeching for crabs and fish,
Deadly lightning severs the sky.
Someone wake me up, I wish, I wish.

Stepping deeper towards the end,
Crispy seaweed hangs from high,
My eye is guided to something in the sand,
I think it's a treasure chest, my oh my.

I clamber over to check it out,
On the front a huge iron lock,
I run my hand across the soggy surface,
It smells as bad as Dad's old sock.

Maybe inside buckets of treasure?
I wrestle to open the wondrous chest,
A reflection of glorious gold hits my eyes,
A lonely stroll turns to a wealthy quest!

Chloe Foot (11)
Blackfield Junior School

HIDDEN TREASURE

I found an egg
What can it be?
A chicken egg?
A goose egg?
What can it be?

When will it hatch?
Today?
Tomorrow?
Wait and see!

I think it's moving!
Oh no
It's only the cat
Wobbling the table.

'Quick Mum, it's hatching!'
What will it be?
A chicken?
A goose?
Wait and see!

It's a . . .
Chicken?
Goose?
No! It's a crocodile!

Clare Cox (9)
Blackfield Junior School

HIDDEN TREASURES

In the sea
Ten metres deep
There was a chest
Which was there to keep

Treasures
Gold, jewels
Everything nice.
No one had seen it, no one at all.

Rebecca Marsden (7)
Blackfield Junior School

HIDDEN TREASURES

You've got to come and check it out,
Because this thing will make you shout.
It's very sparkly and really bright,
If you come and see before it's night.
It might be green, it might be gold,
It might be hot, it might be cold.
You may find it buried in the sand,
You might even find it in the band.
You will have to look far and wide,
It could even be at the seaside.
You've heard that pirates bury their treasure,
But to find it you must be good with your measure.
If you look hard you will see a crown,
But do you look up or do you look down?
The crown belongs to a king,
He has also lost his great big ring.
The king has a brother who is an earl,
Now he used to own a massive pearl.
I've heard that there is a buried chest,
But to find it you will have to be at your best.
Now if you find this hidden chest,
You will have passed this really hard test.
Within the chest is a golden fleece,
But now you may notice the poem does cease.

Rebecca Barker (9)
Blackfield Junior School

HIDDEN TREASURE

Deep in the jungle
I know of a temple that I can take you to
The Incas built it a long time ago
Let's see what we find, you just never know
Treasures of rubies, diamonds and gold
Underground in tombs down in the dark and cold
Rubies of red as red as a rose
Diamonds so large
Gold coins and cups
Hidden treasures from ceiling to floor
Treasures of kings and none for the poor
Snakes and scorpions left there to guard
If only the treasures could speak
And tell us of the past.

Damien Davies (11)
Blackfield Junior School

CREEPY CASTLE

In a castle, dark and dusty,
Stood an armour suit all rusty.
Haunted from breastplate to visor,
Visitors were none the wiser.

Then one day the suit went walking,
Past some tourists who were talking.
How they stared with big, round eyes,
Some let out astonished cries!

'This way, run!' the tour guide said,
And soon everybody fled.

Kelly Hurrell (9)
Blackfield Junior School

HIDDEN TREASURE

H idden treasure
I s hard to find
D eep in the sand, or
D own a spooky mine.
E veryone is wanting to get it, but
N obody can find it.

T o dig up with a spade
R eeling in your reward
E asy to keep to yourself
A lways better to share with two
S ieving through the sand
U nbelieving of what you have found
R icher than you ever dreamed of
E nough to go around.

Joshua Capstick (9)
Blackfield Junior School

HIDDEN TREASURE

A pirate sailed on the high seas,
He jumped off the ship and hurt his knees.
He swam to the island
And found some sand.
In the sand he found a map
Which he rested on his lap.
He read it quickly to find a clue
To find out what he had to do.
With his hands he dug a hole where it said,
Then found the treasures on the seabed.

Keeley Sherred (9)
Blackfield Junior School

HIDDEN TREASURES

There are hidden treasures to be found.
In the sky and on the ground.
A tiny star in a black velvet sky.
A fluffy cloud comes sailing by.
A sunbeam glints on a tiny drop of water
A small pearl hidden in an oyster.

Under the sea hidden from view,
Fishes of all colours big and small,
Seahorses gallop at their own pace
Waving seaweed in the current,
Hiding sea creatures on the seabed.

The large oak tree in the big dark wood,
Holds secrets at the bottom of the trunk,
Little beetles scuttle by, burrowing worms,
Spiders and snails in the leaves.
A new shoot of a plant pops its head through the ground
Life is a treasure I have found.

Rebecca Curtis (11)
Blackfield Junior School

HIDDEN TREASURE

Far away in a chest of drawers,
Lies a treasure close to me,
Nobody walks on the creaky floors,
So no one gets near enough to see.

It's only I who sees the secret,
For it's only I that wears it,
It's only I who wears it on my foot,
Because no one else cares a bit.

Some day someone else will know,
But even they will not know what lies beneath,
Some day someone else will go,
To the chest of drawers but only their visit will be brief,

For now I'll have to go and join the treasure,
But the secret of the treasure will never be known,
And all the people will use the thing for leisure,
But after a while the legend of the ring will be grown.

Jessica Rudd (10)
Blackfield Junior School

HIDDEN TREASURES

Carried by a strong wind
On across the endless sea
To dead man's island
Where treasure is buried under a tree

Ten paces to the north and five paces west
Marks the very spot where the treasure lies at rest.

Hungry eyes and fast hands die
Deeper, wider
Still no sign
Has someone been here before?
Jake has hidden well.

Tomorrow we'll have another go.
Pieces of eight, rubies too.

All this and more.
Someone, somewhere.

Hayley Moore (11)
Blackfield Junior School

HIDDEN TREASURE

On the beach one day
Digging holes in the sand
'A ring,' I call
'Must be treasure' Harry says
Then two men come along
'Quick,' I shout
I put the ring back
The two men dig it up
And take it to a different spot
And put a box in there
They go and we dig it all up
'Gold, silver, in a box?'
'That's my mum's ring,' says Katie
'We'd better take this box to the police,' I say
'Wow!' says Harry
We got a gold piece each
'Well done!' we were told.

Jaime Gemmell (9)
Blackfield Junior School

HIDDEN TREASURE

Hidden treasure
Hidden beneath the slimy seaweed.

Treasure gold
Treasure silver
Treasures round and square.

Treasure in boxes
Treasure in chests
Treasure in an oyster's shell.

Thomas Church (9)
Blackfield Junior School

HIDDEN TREASURE

Up in the attic where nobody goes,
It's full of junk and who knows?
There may be hidden treasures,
Or maybe an old treasure map.
What is this? A loose floorboard
And it is nice and clean with scratches.
I lifted up the floorboard,
My hand digging in the hole,
There was a sweet porcelain doll
And she looked like she was going to a ball.
Then I found ten more - 20, 30, 40.

This was 30 years ago when I was 9
And I still have the dolls.
It seemed like yesterday.

Danielle Parslow (9)
Blackfield Junior School

HIDDEN TREASURES

The treasure is in the sea,
Do not think it's a pea.
The treasure is in a trunk,
Do not think it's a tree trunk.
The treasure is gold,
Do not think it's bold.
There is a jewel,
That is cool.
It's not in the pool.
Where is it?

Ben Brooks (8)
Blackfield Junior School

HIDDEN TREASURE

We were down on the beach playing on the rocks
When we saw a box.
'Maybe it's hidden treasure,' I said to my friend
Then I saw three men coming around the bend.
'Quick, hide,' I said, 'don't make a sound,'
We laid very still on the ground.
The men buried the box then walked away,
We got up from where we lay.
We found the box and home to Dad we dashed,
He opened it up, it was full of cash.
We took the police to the beach where we played,
They caught the crooks the very next day.

Liam Coombs (9)
Blackfield Junior School

HIDDEN TREASURE

A long time ago there lived a girl called Kate,
She went diving for a golden plate,
But all she found was some slate.
When she saw a crab, she picked it up
And it gave her a nip on the lip.
She screamed and landed on a chest.
Kate jumped up with a bump on her head.
Kate picked up the chest
And swam to the surface with a struggle.
Within seconds she was on the beach
With a golden plate with her mate.

Rachel Shrive (10)
Blackfield Junior School

HIDDEN TREASURES

I dug a giant hole,
Too big for a mole.
I dug and dug,
When I got to the bottom,
I saw a little egg.
A leg, stuck out,
Out popped a golden man.
His name was Sam,
He helped me till dawn,
To dig a prawn.
My mum was impressed,
With his hairy chest.
Well, you look rather nice,
Should I make you a cup of spice?

Zeff Hancock (7)
Blackfield Junior School

HIDDEN TREASURE

T reasures are made of gold and silver
R ubies are a deep, blood-red
E meralds are green and shiny
A nd diamonds are the favourite so it's said
S apphires are found in many shades of blue
U nder the sea pearls are hidden in the oyster shells
R ich hidden treasures are there to be found
E ach of us has different treasures
S o if you look carefully you will find your treasures.

Loren Ockelford (8)
Blackfield Junior School

HIDDEN TREASURES

Splash!
We dived into the sea,
We swam down, down, down.
Seaweed was all we could see,
Fish quickly, quietly swam past,
Octopuses also swam past.
Our legs were waving quickly behind us.
We were making hand signs to each other,
'An electric eel! Down there!' I was trying to say.
Suddenly I saw a glint of gold,
I swam towards it,
And there, in the clearing, I could see a treasure chest!
I tried to open it, but it was locked.
I got a stone and tried to open it.
It didn't budge!
My partner and I swam quickly back to the boat.
We grabbed a spanner and dived back in.
When we got to the chest,
We tried to open it with the spanner.
Bang!
The lid flew open!
We were overjoyed!
We took it back up to the boat,
We were going to be rich!
We took it all back to England.
We *were* rich!

Monica Morton (9)
Blackfield Junior School

HIDDEN TREASURE

Down in the jungle depths,
Is where we sent our reps.
The leaves brush on their arms
And also on their palms.
They know the treasure's here,
But they forgot their beer.

Down in the jungle depths,
Is where we sent our reps.
X marks the spot
And they are getting hot.

Down in the jungle depths,
Is where we sent our reps.
Flies are flying all over the place,
There are even bites upon their face.
The reps all miss their beds
And also have itchy heads.

Down in the jungle depths,
Is where we sent our reps.
They have to work in a team,
There's no water to keep them clean.

Down in the jungle depths,
Is where we sent our reps.
Down in the jungle depths,
Is where we lost our *reps!*

Vanessa Sheppard (10)
Blackfield Junior School

HOW I FOUND MY TREASURE

I landed on an island,
an island far out,
so crowded this island,
no voice left to shout.

Full of palm trees,
it is very hot,
Oh! I stepped on something,
it hurts a lot.

Oh my,
am I sure it's what I see?
This box, it's full of treasure,
it's what I see.

My heart, it's racing,
beat! Beat! Beat!
It's good I didn't have to dig
or I'd be fried in the heat.

I'm so amazed,
I'm finally in luck,
so cool,
I'll write in my diary.

What's the point
silly me,
of having treasure,
if there's nowhere to go, and I'm surrounded by sea?

Lucy Wainwright (10)
Blackfield Junior School

HIDDEN TREASURES

Hidden treasure, hidden treasure
Pirates come to find it,
Hidden treasure, hidden treasure
You find it in the sea.

Hidden treasure, hidden treasure
In between the seaweed.
Hidden treasure, hidden treasure
Shiny and gold.

Hidden treasure, hidden treasure
You can buy a lot with it.
Hidden treasure, hidden treasure
It's money before your eyes.

Hidden treasure, hidden treasure
It's a chest full of gold,
Hidden treasure, hidden treasure
Pirates fight for it.

Hidden treasure, hidden treasure
I'm the craftiest pirate who sailed
The seven seas.
Hidden treasure, hidden treasure,
Blackbeard's my name.

Hidden treasure, hidden treasure
Other pirates fear me most.
Hidden treasure, hidden treasure
It's all mine, mine, mine!

Charlotte Pilcher (9)
Blackfield Junior School

HIDDEN TREASURES

One summer's day,
Everyone was out to play.

'Let's go somewhere.'
'Where, where, where?'

'Follow me
And wait and see.'

'So where are we going first?'
'Somewhere where you'll pop and burst.'

So they went to and fro.
'Now where are we going to go?'

'To explore.'
'No, no, no, I don't really want to go.'

'Come and see what I've found.'
'Wait, I'm spinning all around.'
'I've found treasure! Yippee!'

Teri Thomas (8)
Blackfield Junior School

HIDDEN TREASURES

Hidden treasures in the park,
Hidden treasures under bark,
Hidden treasures under a chair,
Hidden treasures everywhere.

On the beach,
Or out of reach,
Maybe in the soft sand,
They could be anywhere on the land.

They could be in lots of trees,
They could be stuck on the leaves,
Lots of them have lots of measures,
Can you find the hidden treasures?

Hollie Jones (9)
Blackfield Junior School

HIDDEN TREASURES

Within the forbidden forest
Beyond the fields of corn
Lies my hidden treasure
The snow-white unicorn.

Her coat is so soft -
Her eyes are so bright
Here lies my hidden treasure
In the evening light.

Her mane of shimmering silver
Her horn of glittering gold
This is my hidden treasure
That makes legends of old.

Beneath the cool shade
She finds a new home
You can find my hidden treasure
Where she can safely roam.

Within the forbidden forest
Beyond the fields of corn
Lies my hidden treasure
The snow-white unicorn.

Claire Todd (7)
Blackfield Junior School

HIDDEN TREASURE

I am a diver
Looking for treasure
It is my hobby
It gives me pleasure

Swimming in the sea
Looking for gold
Searching and searching
Until I'm too old

I had better hide
I see sharks coming this way
Powerful and fierce
Hunting and searching for prey

Diving into a sea cave
To my surprise
I see a twinkling
I had found my prize.

It's treasure!

Stephanie Hughes (9)
Blackfield Junior School

HIDDEN TREASURE

There's hidden treasure to find.
What could it be behind?
I'm looking for treasure.
It will give me so much pleasure.

Ruby rings, diamonds and crowns,
All those people who don't try are clowns.
Could it be behind a palm tree?
If I find it people will love me!

I'll buy a country for myself,
Get a servant to clean my golden shelf.
Money! Money! Money!
Just like honey.

I could be a millionaire!
I could have a golden pair of underwear!
I would be cool, funky and hip,
I could have a cruise ship.

Melissa Bainbridge (9)
Blackfield Junior School

HIDDEN TREASURE

What treasures are there in the world?
There's silver, bronze and gold.
But the greatest treasures are the hidden ones
And can never be bought or sold.

The biggest of these hidden treasures
Cannot be locked in a castle store,
But was placed inside all children's hearts,
Where it will grow forever more.

It is the oldest treasure in the world,
Far better than the favourite toy.
It is the same across all countries
And for every girl and boy.

I don't know where it came from,
Or when it first began,
Or who decided to give it a name,
But I know, I call it fun.

Alex Williams (9)
Blackfield Junior School

TREASURE

Treasure is cool
Treasure is good
Treasure is fun to find.

You can find it at the place marked X
You can find it at the bottom of the sea
You can find it by a tree
In the garden or even in your home.

Treasure can be all sorts of things
Mums that make you well
Gems, gold and silver jewels
That special toy, that rag you had as a baby.

Treasure is what you want it to be
Treasure is cool
Treasure is good
Treasure is fun to find.

Lee Hutchings (10)
Blackfield Junior School

HIDDEN TREASURE

I'm looking for some lovely gold,
Buried in the sand.
Can you help me?
I need a helping hand.

If I could wish for something new,
It would be for gold.
I've wished and wished and wished,
For the thing I've just told.

This lovely gold,
I've just told,
Might not be in this sand,
It could be in another land.

Vicki Wilkinson (9)
Blackfield Junior School

MY DREAM

Last night was the greatest experience to be,
I never noticed my hidden treasure was in front of me.
I searched through the jungle,
I searched through the sea,
When my treasure was right in front of me.

It comes at night,
All year round,
Can come in day,
But very rarely found.

It can be scary,
It can be strange,
It can be fun
But it can be weird.

In my hidden treasure you may be
Very brave and strong.
But then again you may be
Very weak and scared.

My hidden treasure is to be
My dream.

Leanne Cox (10)
Blackfield Junior School

THE PAINTING

The tigers lie in the long grass, still
Looking as if they could kill.
A snake appears, slithering along,
Hissing his warning song.

A pure white dove sits high on a tree,
Looking as far as he can see.
Below the jungle is shades of green,
The animals are all so mean.

As I stare at this painting,
My heart starts to sing,
How come I never see
This beauty in front of me?

James Scaum (10)
Blackfield Junior School

HIDDEN TREASURE

T   reasure hidden in the sand
R   otten chest, hard lid
E   xciting crown in the chest
A   colourful chest
S   erves you right if you didn't find it
U   nder the sea
R   ubies in the chest
E   xtremely sparkly
S   unken treasure.

Jessica Davis (7)
Blackfield Junior School

HIDDEN TREASURES

I put on my aqualung,
I plunge to the depths
And down and down I go.
I see a jellyfish,
I don't touch it
Because I would get stung.

Then beside me
There is a green turtle.
It swims and swims
Like nothing I've seen.

I see the bright colours
Of purple and green,
From the colours of fish, coral
And other hidden treasures of the sea.

Decca Brooks (10)
Blackfield Junior School

HIDDEN TREASURE

Hidden treasure beneath the deep,
As I go along, I hear whales cry,
Deeper I go and there I see a starfish lie.

There's my, only my treasure,
The golden coins, rings and jewellery await me.
Finally, my destiny is unravelled
But yet it is a bunch of measly bits of seaweed.

Daniel Tonkin (10)
Blackfield Junior School

THE HIDDEN TREASURE

I walked upon the creaky boat,
I passed the old, tall mast,
Quickly, I went in a door
And then I ran out fast.

In the door was a huge and scary,
Fat and hairy, enormous spider!
I nearly fainted, what a shock,
But something behind it - a big, golden lock!

I very quietly looked again,
I had to take a rest,
It shocked me to see such a thing,
A golden treasure chest!

How will I get it?
I thought for a sec,
But then I saw it,
A sword on the deck.

I ran towards the sparkling sword,
Aha, I thought, this will kill it,
This will kill the spider's life,
Bit by bit by bit.

I went along to the door again,
I tiptoed slowly inside,
Then slash, slash, slash, with all my horror,
The spider slowly died.

I skipped along to the gleaming chest,
I had never felt so happy,
Inside the chest was a lovely bird,
With orange wings so flappy.

I love this bird, I thought to myself,
I will keep him as a pet,
He will be the best bird ever,
I'll love him forever, I bet.

Beckie Noon (9)
Blackfield Junior School

HIDDEN TREASURES

Diamond-blue sea twinkling in the midday sun,
No one around except a special someone.
Swimming with a splash, a mermaid caught my eye,
Swimming with her dolphin friends, she gave a bored sigh.
All of a sudden the mermaid saw a sparkle in the golden sand,
With excitement she took my hand.
She led me down full of glee,
Through the waters of the deep blue sea.
We swam over coral and through tropical fish,
Where we met an octopus who gave us a wish.
We saw a sparkle that was as clear as ice,
I think our treasure chest was so nice.
We swam back to shore to see what we had,
Our treasure was so exciting, we were so glad.
With prizes so pretty, I couldn't believe,
This amazing adventure I had under the sea.
I went home to see Mum and Dad,
To show them my hidden treasure tucked in my bag.

Laura Delaney (8)
Blackfield Junior School

HIDDEN TREASURE

Getting in,
Diving down,
With my buddy, Lyn.

Diving down,
It's getting creepy,
Lots of shadows,
Quiet and sleepy.

What's that over there?
What could it be?
Is it a fish
Or is it just me?

I found a box,
I opened its lid.
As I looked down,
I saw pearls sparkling.

Gemma Skeggs (10)
Blackfield Junior School

HIDDEN TREASURE

Running through the jungle,
Swinging from tree to tree,
I look for something special,
I look for treasure.

Plunging deep into the sea,
I see lots of seaweed,
There is also the feel of the sand,
No treasure here either.

As I bob to the surface,
I suddenly realise something,
I don't need treasure,
All I need is family, friends and animals.

Joanne Hayward (10)
Blackfield Junior School

HIDDEN TREASURE

A long time ago
In a far-off land
Treasure was buried
Under the sand.

The island was a loner
The trees grew in lines
For the island had been deserted
For a very long time.

The island was found
By a very famous man
But the treasure still lay buried
Beneath a leafy fan.

The island became a holiday place
Sand, sea and sun
A once quiet and lonely place
Was now a place for fun.

Still the secret was unfound
The treasure remained well hid
No one was going to find
What was sealed beneath that lid!

Chrissie Morris (10)
Blackfield Junior School

HIDDEN TREASURES

What's your hidden treasure?
Mine's my family.
They are always there when I am down,
To put some cheer in me.

My mum and dad are happy,
They always make me laugh,
If I have a problem,
I know who I should ask.

When we go on long walks,
We have lots of fun,
Getting dirty, chasing the dogs,
While spending time with Dad and Mum.

I love it at dinner time,
When we all sit around the table,
We laugh and joke and talk a lot
And eat as much as we are able.

When we go to bed at night,
I feel cosy and content,
Because I know my family love me,
As much as I love them.

I know that I am lucky,
As some children do not have this,
And every day I am grateful,
That my family live in bliss.

These are my hidden treasures,
Though not for all to see,
They may not be material,
But they are treasures dear to me.

Hannah Poole (10)
Blackfield Junior School

HIDDEN TREASURE

Down I go,
For a quick little peek,
But I don't know
What I would seek.

A shipwreck,
Or glittering gold,
I find on my trek,
For a story untold.

On I go,
Throughout the sea,
Going high and low,
A treasure for me.

But there a shell,
What I could see,
Is what I would tell,
As a treasure for me.

I dive down deep,
To pick it up,
For that's what I'd keep,
To give me good luck.

I broke through the top,
To find people everywhere,
Looking at what I'd got
And giving me a stare.

It's an ordinary shell,
People might say and see,
But as I would tell,
It's precious to me!

Melissa Hawkins (10)
Blackfield Junior School

HIDDEN TREASURE

Can you find the hidden treasure?
Yes, that would be such a pleasure.

I looked at the map
And put on my sailor cap.

I headed out to sea
With a sailor singing merrily.

I found an island and went ashore,
Shells and pebbles covered the floor.

I looked here and I looked there,
But I couldn't find it anywhere.

I walked around to where X marked the spot,
By that time I was boiling hot.

Then I found the hidden treasure
And it was a great pleasure.

Samantha Ball (7)
Blackfield Junior School

BURIED TREASURE

The pirate looks at paper
And X marks the spot.
He looks for buried treasure
And hopes it's quite a lot.

He takes a spade
And digs for gold,
In a box he finds a book
With stories to be told.

The pirate looks at paper
And X marks the spot.
He's very disappointed
A book is all he's got
And he never learnt to read.

Kayleigh Taylor (10)
Blackfield Junior School

HIDDEN TREASURE

Under the water, in the sea,
there lies a treasure box waiting to be seen.
Treasure takes all kinds of form,
it could even be hidden in the new forest storm.

Treasure holds all kinds of things,
it might carry golden rings.
It's a shame nobody can find it,
we don't know what wonders are held.

Treasure could be guarded by scary things,
well, we might become rich.
Maybe the treasure won't be guarded
by a terrifying witch.

Treasure is not just golden rings,
nor is it shiny things.
My treasure isn't guarded by any nasty things,
it isn't my teddy or my swing.
I found my treasure long ago,
it's my family and I love them so.

Matthew Sait (9)
Blackfield Junior School

HIDDEN TREASURE

Happy feelings
are being with your friends.

Happy feelings
are getting what you really want.

Happy feelings
are going somewhere new.

Happy feelings
are winning a competition.

Happy feelings
are inventing new things.

Happy feelings
are when you are a year older.

Sarah Kate Jones (8)
Blackfield Junior School

HIDDEN TREASURES

There once was a chest of treasure,
marked on the lid with a feather.

The chest was full of gold,
when the pirates found it they felt very happy and bold.

When lifting the chest of treasure,
their backs nearly broke with the pressure.

Then they all ended up in a hospital bed
and didn't get up forever.

Jade Hawkins (7)
Blackfield Junior School

HIDDEN TREASURE

I'm going to find the hidden treasure,
but only at my own leisure.
Down deep I'll go into the sea,
and find unknown people, maybe.

My mermaid friends will help me look
even if five hours we took.
Deeper we go into the sea and more fish
we see. The water is as clean as fresh
water in a dish, clear enough for
tons of fish.

As we reach the sunken ship,
all just having a little sip,
We swim right in and find a key,
maybe that opens the treasure for me.

Laura Moody (9)
Blackfield Junior School

HIDDEN TREASURES

Once I found some hidden treasure
It brought me lots of pleasure
There were loads and loads of hidden gems
They looked like lots of multicoloured pens
I dug them up on a big, big beach
I took them home and washed them with bleach
They were as sparkly as could be
They were all you could see
I liked them very, very much
I kept them in a large hutch.

Zoe Hanley (9)
Blackfield Junior School

HIDDEN TREASURE

Down I dive,
Deeper, deeper.
For I am a treasure seeker,
I approach my goal in stealth.

Deeper I push and spot the bottom,
I glide along the ocean floor,
Seeking my treasure,
Seeking a long-lost locked door.

I find my eyes locked on some weeds,
I see many small shells, like golden beads.
Slowly I flow towards them,
Slowly I lift off the weeds,
Slowly I pick up my treasure,
Slowly I swim up to the surface - in joy.

Eliot Tibbit (10)
Blackfield Junior School

MY METAL DETECTOR

I went walking along the beach
With my metal detector by my feet
I was hoping I would find
Lots of treasure of different kinds.

Beep, beep, beep, dig, dig, dig
The hole I dug was so deep
All I found, rusty and round
Was a pound
But looking for this buried treasure
Was great fun and lots of pleasure.

Katy Bird (7)
Blackfield Junior School

HIDDEN TREASURES

The treasures under the ocean deep,
Glistens below the surface,
The tiny crab creeps out for a peep,
Its shell streaked with crystal lace.

A starfish clings to a rocky ledge
All crimson and aquamarine,
One moves around a coral hedge,
So slowly it's hardly seen.

A little deeper the scallop lies
Its shell an exquisite fan,
These treasures go about their lives
All hidden from the eyes of man.

Hazel Katie Pugh (10)
Blackfield Junior School

HIDDEN TREASURES

Ten miles down where no humans have been,
Lies glistening coral that no one has seen.
With colourful seaweed swaying in the seas,
Like a giant oak tree in a gentle breeze.

No one can measure up to the deep blue sea,
No matter how clever you think you can be.
The deep, deep sea is always the best,
With its sparkling pearls always at rest.

Such beauty beneath, you cannot measure,
The deep blue sea's hidden treasure!

Kerry Allen (10)
Blackfield Junior School

MY CAT

The sleek and shiny fur
Of my black and white cat,
Looks like squares on a chessboard.
He's called KitKat!

His eyes are green,
Not brown or blue
And sometimes, but not always
He sleeps in my shoe!

His tail is long
Sways to and fro,
And if you touch it,
He scratches your toe!

His whiskers are thin
Twitchy and white,
But if you knock them,
He might give you a bite!

My cat is special,
Well he is to me.
Oh my gosh,
I forgot to give him his tea!

But I know,
He will always love me.

Tiffany Heasman (11)
Foundry Lane Primary School

DRUGS

Drugs are bad
They make you go mad.
They are good as medicine, if you take the amount suggested,
So that they can get digested.

Drugs are bad and you know it,
I can tell you this, though I'm a poet.
I cannot tell you what to do,
But I suggest you flush them down the loo!

Rachel Vear (10)
Foundry Lane Primary School

MY FRIENDS

When my friends and I walk to school
We like talking about things that are cool

I really like it when my friends come
round to play
Especially when it is a nice sunny day

We lay on the grass, looking to the sky
Watching the puffy clouds go sailing by

We giggle and talk about things that we've done
Whilst we lay back and soak up the bright
yellow sun

Having someone to share a secret with,
Knowing they will
Never tell
And someone to phone when you are not
Feeling well

My friends I will treasure, I will miss them
When they're gone
Just like the sun, if it never ever shone.

Jennifer Platt (11)
Foundry Lane Primary School

THE CAT

My cat is really quite daft
He runs like a giraffe
He will chase your car whether you go near or far.

At night he wrestles the carpet and eats melon from the market.
When people walk past, he smacks them quite fast.

He's hard to ignore as he nibbles and dribbles
His way through the hedge and under the garden shed.

Although he wouldn't win any prizes,
We enjoy his many disguises,
And he never ceases to surprise us.

Seth Dismore (10)
Foundry Lane Primary School

MY MATE CALLED MOLE

My favourite toy 'Moley'
He is now old and holey,
I take him to bed,
He listens to every word that's said.
He seems to be in my dreams night and day,
I would hate it if he got taken away.
I sometimes take him to school
Which could be against the rule.
My friends would like him to play
But I quickly put him away,
I would like him to last,
As he is part of my past.

Ben Candy (10)
Foundry Lane Primary School

NATURE'S FEELINGS

What is lightning?
Nature's firework display.
What is a tornado?
A raging tower of death.
What is an earthquake?
The pathway to Hell's chambers.
What is snow?
A purifying blanket.
What is the wind?
An invisible force of harmony
and destruction.
What is the rain?
Nature's tears of sorrow.
What is the sky?
The endless roof of the world.
What is the sun?
The blinking light of the universe.
What is the fog?
Nature's secretive mist.

Joanna Wroe (11)
Foundry Lane Primary School

PRAYING MANTIS

Beautiful but deadly,
Predator waiting for its prey
And saying its grace.
Then in an instant it hooks,
The prey can not escape now.

Ryan Williams (11)
Foundry Lane Primary School

BEN THE DOG

It's not fair, I can't have a dog
Goldfish are always the same,
Swimming around their log
Stick insects are really quite tame,
From their brambles, they simply suspend.

Puppies, you can take for a walk,
You can't take your fish to the park.
My mum has just had a talk,
With my neighbour who's called Mr Mark,
They have just had a new dog called Ben.

Celine Galloway (11)
Foundry Lane Primary School

WHAT IS WEATHER? GOD'S CREATION

What is thunder?
A big man strolling down the street.

What is rain?
A waterfall rushing down into the sea below.

What is snow?
A bit of cotton on the ground.

What is wind?
God whistling when he's walking around Heaven.

Joseph Mark Fuccio (11)
Foundry Lane Primary School

DOGS

Dogs bark all day long
Even when midnight's gone
Keeping all the neighbours up
They always say 'He's just a pup'

In the morning, eating food
He laps up his, then eats yours too!

Years on, when he's all grown up
You'll find the neighbours won't stay up
They'll always say they miss his bark
But they'll stop and think, he's rather smart.

Laura Finlay (11)
Foundry Lane Primary School

THE ROLLING WEATHER

What is the snow?
Flour being spilled.
What is the rainbow?
Paints being poured in line
What is thunder?
God moving furniture.
What is the sky?
Shapes being drawn on blue paper.
What is the sun?
A torch through the clouds.

Danielle Wateridge (10)
Foundry Lane Primary School

WEATHERS WONDERFUL EMOTIONS

What is the sun?
All the stars uniting to create a radiator for the shivering sky

What is rain?
God spitting in disgust when the world misbehaves

What is a tornado?
A spiralling staircase accompanying people to Heaven

What is snow?
God's comforting duvet carpeting the enchanted Earth

What is a tidal wave?
A deep bath, violently overflowing onto the unsuspecting universe

What is lightning?
God unexpectedly reminding us of his immense power

What are hailstones?
God furiously hurling glass marbles at the gullible civilians of Earth

What is fog?
The steam from God's shower, creating a secretive mist

What is thunder?
God's lonely stomach signalling it is in need of company

What is a rainbow?
Colours randomly being splattered on to the sky,
creating a unique piece of art.

Stephanie Millard (11)
Foundry Lane Primary School

My Memory

This is memory
This is all my memory
It makes you happy
It might make you unhappy
But this is my memory.

Anzu Suzuki (10)
Foundry Lane Primary School

What I Can See . . .

The late night traffic
And the stones lying
breathless
Leaves fall from the trees
The light skimming from
windows
And the dark clouds are
fading.

Liam Davis (10)
Foundry Lane Primary School

The Whistle Of The Wind

The wind blows gently picking up every sweeping leaf,
It takes it up until all is still,
The whistle gets louder as you walk towards the empty air,
The mighty whistle of the wind.

Michelle Martin (11)
Foundry Lane Primary School

NEVER MESS WITH LIONS!

'Never mess with lions!'
My granny always says
But I just took it for a joke
Until the other day.

Drinking toilet water
Was a lion in the bathroom
I chatted for a while
And then I met my doom.

First it ripped my head off
And sucked out all my guts
It was then that I realised
That this was more than just a cut.

But the hospital *can* do wonders
So they stitched me all back up
So remember
Never mess with lions!

Lucy Argall (10)
Highfield CE Primary School

MY SISTER

I have a younger sister
who's just like me
we look and sound the same
and it really annoys me.

My parents get muddled up
when we are talking to them
they think it's my sister
when it is really me.

My sister's really annoying
nothing like me
she gets into grumpy moods
but is usually crazy.

Yes, my sister's annoying
even her friends agree
but still she's my sister
and I love her as much as she loves *me*.

Chiara Wall (9)
Highfield CE Primary School

WAR FROM THE POPPIES POINT OF VIEW

We try to push through, through the dead bodies
We try to help you relive your life again,
We try to make the last moment of your life happy,
We try to help.

But how can we? For even though the enemy committed a crime
You and they will never forget,
You also did the same, for you both killed someone.
But we will still try and remember
That before the war took over your mind,
You were innocent.
And of course, your country was depending on you all.

But you can't forget; you can't undo anything and you can't unkill!
So next time you go to war, think before you waste your bullets
And think before you waste your life.

Catherine Jones (9)
Highfield CE Primary School

POEMS

Poems are complicated things,
Should they rhyme or not?
It's far too hard for me
They tie my brain in a knot!

What should I write about?
The seasons or the moon?
Fruits, plants even Timbuktu.

But I guess in a strange sort of way,
Poems are elegant things,
To read in your head or to say
So you can decide for me,
And tell me what you think
Okay?

Sophie Sayer (10)
Highfield CE Primary School

THE FAT RABBIT

There was a rabbit,
Who had a habit,
Of eating all day.
Eating and eating made him fat,
So he put on his thinking hat,
And called Mrs Clever Cat.
Mrs Clever Cat gave him good advise,
So he started to do some exercise.
He started to run,
And have some fun.
After a week he was much thinner,
And started having sensible dinner.

Shreya Chugh (8)
Highfield CE Primary School

MY DOLPHIN

I was riding on a dolphin when it suddenly smiled at me,
It paddled with its fins and swam right out to sea.

First we passed a whale, which could have got me in a gulp,
But my dolphin saved us both from being squashed into a pulp.

Next we saw the piranhas; their little teeth were bared,
Who would have gone near them? I wouldn't have dared!

Then came the great white shark, its teeth were bright, bright white,
It was searching through the deep blue sea for an early morning bite.

But again my little dolphin bravely saved the day,
By shooting like a little star out of the sharkie's way!

I'd had enough by now, 'Please dolphin, no more!'
So my superb young dolphin swam me safely to the shore.

Rachel Guyer (10)
Highfield CE Primary School

A NONSENSE POEM

A large, fluffy, furry beast,
has just come in my house to finish out feast.
He's scary and frightening, he's as fast as lightning!
He's eating that feast like there is no tomorrow,
I bet he would be good to follow!
I followed him over hills and rocks,
But then we bumped into a big bad fox.
That fox, he said to me, 'Did you know that's a cat!'
I said, 'What? No it's not!'
So I took a good look and said, 'You're a crook!
Scaring people like that, now go and say sorry you silly cat!'

Megan Hoskins (9)
North Baddesley Junior School

ON THE FLOOR . . .

I can see on the floor,
A bright copper teapot,
Love at home is its name,
Whose can it be?

It's definitely not mine,
Don't think it's my mum's,
Maybe it's Dad's,
Whose can it be?

It's littered with flowers,
And birds like great peacocks,
Those curly horned rams,
Whose can it be?

My brother's come in,
He's just disappeared,
Come back with a blanket,
What does this mean?

It's now in a blanket,
Wrapped up in a ball,
Ben says that it's his,
What else does he need?

Elise Cox (9)
North Baddesley Junior School

CATS

Fluffy, furry ball of fluff,
Tearing, chewing, quite rough.
Sleeping, eyes shut, make no sound,
Purring, twitching, running around.

Cuddling, curling on your lap,
Then getting sleepy so she has a nap!
Snoring a little too loud,
She is asleep now, so make no sound.

Harriet Baker (9)
North Baddesley Junior School

TIME

Time goes tick-tock all your life,
You can never turn back time,
Time is a thing that will never die,
You've got to have fun in the time that you're given,
Time is a thing that will never stop.

Gemma Parker (10)
North Baddesley Junior School

OUTSIDE MY WINDOW

Outside my window a family of deer I see.
The deer are as scared as mice.
Their enemy, the big bison.
The deer are as frightened as fish.
The daddy deer as brave as a lion.
Trying his best to protect his family.
The stream flowing peacefully along.

Jessica Knight (9)
North Baddesley Junior School

MY SCARY DOG

I can see a horrible monster coming towards me
Oh, how I wished he couldn't see
Help! I hope Mum comes if I scream
This monster looks really mean
I heard him scratch on the door
I think he's going to *roar!*
I really hope he doesn't see me
When I hide in the cupboard
I didn't think he would look there
Like Mother Hubbard
It's a shadow, who could it be?
I can't really see
It's my dog
With a log
He isn't scary.

Sasha Hunt (9)
North Baddesley Junior School

THROUGH MY BINOCULARS

Through my binoculars,
I can see a serious eagle,
His sharp, bony claws hung tight onto the tree branch.
The angry eagle is as still as a statue.
The fast eagle flies straight down,
Whiz, whiz, whiz, *crash!*
The eagle gobbles the mice in one bite.
The silhouette of an eagle is as sharp as a pin.
The beak as curled as the claw of a leopard.
Sunlight like a big, round, shiny ball,
Shining down on the fierce, angry eagle.

Karmen Tang (9)
North Baddesley Junior School

SEASONS

Spring
Daffodils and crocus erupting with a shower of colour,
Lambs skipping happily over sunny green fields,
Whilst birds chirp musically in the trees.

Summer
Warm air like spices you can almost taste,
Children playing on a sandy beach,
Salty water lapping up against your legs.

Autumn
A cold windy blast blowing through your hair
And shaking the trees above,
Golden leaves rustling and the branches are almost bare.

Winter
Icy coldness and snow that falls like big white balls of cotton wool,
Silence surrounds me as my warm breath creates
A huge fog in front of my eyes!

Catherine Airey (10)
North Baddesley Junior School

THE RIVER

Running rapidly, turning and twisting, the river is coming
Speedily sprinting, crashing clumsily, the river is coming
Slyly striding, flowing cautiously, the river continues
Slithering slowly, powerful and strong, the river continues
Everlasting and endlessly, the mighty river has come to its end
Deadly and dangerously the forceful river has come to its end.

Ben Tugwell (10)
Sarisbury CE Junior School

LIKES AND HATES

What I like about football is I get all muddy
And it is great fun.

What I hate about football is
When the other team tackles me.

What I like about football is when
I score a goal and when I
Tackle the other team.

What I hate about football is when
It is sunny and too hot.

What I hate about football is when
My team loses against the
Other team.

What I like about football is it is
On the TV all of the time.

What I hate about football is when
The other team scores a great goal.

Adam Petyt (7)
Sarisbury CE Junior School

SKATEBOARDS

What I hate about skateboards is
their wheels come off,
What I like about skateboards is
they can do lots of tricks,
What I hate about skateboards is
they always get broken,
What I like about skateboards is
they can be kept in the garage.

What I hate about skateboards is
they have small wheels,
What I like about skateboards is
they can do the slope,
What I hate about skateboards is
people always fall off them.

Daniel Saunders (7)
Sarisbury CE Junior School

HAMSTERS

What I hate about hamsters is
they make the cage dirty every day.
What I like about hamsters is
they are sweet and cute and
they tickle me.

What I hate about hamsters is
they bite me when I clean them out.
What I like about hamsters is
I can feed them every day and every week.

What I hate about hamsters is
that my hamsters fight over their food
every day.
What I like about hamsters is
that they hug me when I pick them up
sometimes.

What I hate about hamsters is
they are sometimes horrible to me.
What I like about hamsters is
that they come out at night.

Gabriella Alberti (7)
Sarisbury CE Junior School

RIVERS

T here are lots of me scattered around
H ear me crash against the rocks
E veryone comes to visit me.

R eally I am wet
I am a sly little pie
V iew my pets under me
E xamples of me around the world
R iver's my name and drowning is my game

T ake a chance with me, like everyone does
E veryone loves me
S ee me coming and swim
T alking to me, everyone loves to do.

Stuart Franklin (9)
Sarisbury CE Junior School

THE RIVER NILE

T he River Nile
H iding hiccups
E normous echoes

R ocky river
I ncredibly deep
V iscious hunters
E normous echoes
R ocky river

N asty Nile
I ncredibly deep
L istening levers
E normous echoes.

Danielle Hudson (10)
Sarisbury CE Junior School

RIVERS

T he River Thames is like a puzzle
H as rocks and meanders like a maze
E very river has its own name, like a person.

R iver Thames runs around London like a letter
I t eventually makes its own way to the mouth
V ery hard storms hit the River Thames like a black night
E very thing is the same as in normal countries to the River Thames
R iver Thames is one of the longest rivers, like a road

T ributaries are included in the River Thames, like a tail on a dog
H as a lot of transport passing through, like a tunnel
A nd it gets creatures swimming on it like a boat.
M ost people don't find the River Thames interesting - like pets.
E very creature which comes along, stays there.
S ome unusual rivers, do not have tributaries, like people.

Christie Jarman (9)
Sarisbury CE Junior School

THE LAKE

A lake, long, wide and departed from the river
full of creatures, insects, fish and plants.
Though the depth is dangerous, the rest
holds great beauty and safeness.
It loves nature, tries to help
be as friendly as possible
It ripples and waves, shakes and stirs
reflecting sun and moon in beautiful light
It's Mother Nature's most reliable and
trustworthy friend.

Adam White (9)
Sarisbury CE Junior School

RIVERS

T here are lots of me scattered around
H ear me crash against the rocks
E veryone comes to bathe in me

R eally everyone says I'm wet
I am like a sly little pie
V iew my sparkles and gleams
E xamples of me are in Atlases
R iver is my name, drowning is my game

T ake charge of me, everyone does
E veryone loves me
S ee me, come in and swim
T alk to me everyone loves to do it.

Ellen Smith (9)
Sarisbury CE Junior School

RIVERS

Rivers can be cold
  Some rivers have meanders
    The River Thames has meanders
      The river goes splash, splash
        The rivers of the sea go
          Splash! Splash!
        The coldness of the river is
      As the coldness of the sea
    You can see the river there
  For years and years
  The rivers go
Splish! Splash!

Amanda Gray (10)
Sarisbury CE Junior School

RIVERS

I am a stream,
  I start by the rain on top of a mountain
    I sometimes make floods,
      I run down the road, day and night
      I like my stream because
          People get a drink from me
            But now I have to change
              I am a river.
              People swim in me, day by day
            When I grow older and reach the sea
          People will fish in me,
        Now I have reached the sea
      I am the sea,
I have fish swimming in me, day and night,
Being the sea is best.

Robin Smith (9)
Sarisbury CE Junior School

THE RAIN POEM

What I like about rain is that you can splash in big wet puddles.
What I hate about the rain is that you get very wet.
What I like about rain is that when rains and the sun comes out,
it makes a rainbow.
What I hate about the rain is that you can fall in it.
What I like about the rain is when it is pitter pattering on the roof.
What I hate about the rain is that you cannot go outside to play.
What I like about the rain is that it helps flowers grow.
What I hate about the rain is that it makes your cat or dog wet.
What I like about the rain is that it drips off the leaves.

Christie Barber (7)
Sarisbury CE Junior School

LIKES AND HATES

What I like about pandas
Is that the young cubs
Sleep in a round, little ball
And they eat bamboo, which is good for them.

What I hate about rats
Is the way they follow you with those
Sly, beady eyes so you get really
Annoyed and angry and awful.

What I like about rabbits
Is that their ears are very
Silky, so you can give them a feel
And the way they bound up and down for fun.

What I hate about snakes
Is the way they slide around in the grass
So silently that you can't hear them, so they sneak out
And *bite you!* That would be a very bad thing to happen.

What I like about chinchillas
Is that they are grey and can jump
Sometimes if they want to
And how they sleep, with their short, little tails poking out.

What I hate about the zoo is
The way the keepers leave the animals in
Such a bad way, so that loads of people make fun of them
And how they make the animals tame and make them do tricks.

Dominic Short (8)
Sarisbury CE Junior School

LIKES AND HATES

What I like about Hammy my hamster
Is that he is playful and I like the way he plays
On the top of his ball.

What I hate about boys
Is that they are noisy and annoying.

What I like about my bed
Is that you can cuddle up and go to sleep.

What I hate about clocks
Is that they wake me up early in the morning.

What I like about snow
Is you can build a snowman then jump on it.

What I hate about wind
Is it can blow trees down and block you in.

What I like about art
Is you can get all messy.

What I hate about bananas
Is they always have lines on.

What I like about my teacher,
Is she mostly helps me when I'm stuck.

What I hate about homework
Is it takes too long.

Mollie Taylor (7)
Sarisbury CE Junior School

LIKES AND HATES

What I like about swimming is
that you can do what you want -
like jumping off the diving board
and going in a rubber hoop, play
with the floats and jump in and
do a roly-poly.

What I hate about swimming is
that you have to swim ten metres
up and down without stopping to have a
break and you have to go right to the bottom
in the deep end and stay down there for
twenty-five seconds.

What I like about swimming is
that you can go on the floating stepping
stones and the floating frogs or the
big float with holes in.

What I hate about swimming is
you get told off when you go underwater
when you're not supposed to and when
you stop in the middle of the pool.

What I like about swimming is
when you get to wear flippers at fun night
and you can play splash the shark.

Chloe Prebble (8)
Sarisbury CE Junior School

LIKES AND HATES

What I like about cats
is how they have cute, little, furry faces and how they purr
loudly and how they curl up.

What I hate about slugs
is that they eat all your plants
and they are slimy and have a horrible colour.

What I like about cats
is how they catch my feet under the warm,
cosy, snugly bed covers.

What I hate about stick insets
is that they crawl along and make you jump
when you don't expect it to happen.

What I like about cats
is how their little voices make you laugh
and how they try to stay awake when they're
falling into a dreamy sleep.

What I hate about rats
is that they spread disease and how they live
in your smelly, dirty, disgusting rubbish bins.

What I like about cats
is how they drink and purr at the same time
and how they play around with warm, fluffy wool.

Jennifer Carson-Paul (8)
Sarisbury CE Junior School

LIKES AND HATES

What I like about rabbits
Is they're soft, cuddly and cute.
What I hate about rabbits
Is their sharp claws and they scratch you.

What I like about chocolate
Is the way it tastes so good.
What I hate about chocolate
Is that it's very tempting to eat.

What I like about my teacher
Is when I'm stuck, she helps me,
What I hate about my teacher is
She makes me do hard work.

What I like about the sun
Is that you can relax.
What I hate about the sun
Is you get burned and have to put cream on.

Tamara Goddard (7)
Sarisbury CE Junior School

THE HORROR OF THE GRAVEYARD

Something wanders through the graveyard,
It makes the creaks and groans,
You cannot ignore the presence,
Of these terrible, gruesome moans.

Does it only live here
To give people a scare?
Oh no! The gates are closed
By the horror that lives there.

There's something here
I know it!
But what I don't know
Its face is hidden always.
It does not want to show.

Daniel Wilson (8)
Sarisbury CE Junior School

LIKES AND HATES

What I like about a pineapple
is that it is all deliciously juicy inside.
What I hate about a pineapple
is all the prickly spikes round the edge.

What I like about a pineapple
is it is all very beautifully soft inside.
What I hate about a pineapple
is it has lots of little brown seeds inside.

What I like about glitter
is it sparkles so brightly at night-time.
What I hate about glitter
is that it is very fiddly to put on
sticky glue.

What I like about glitter
is that it makes me feel all relaxed
and gentle.
What I hate about glitter
is that my mummy complains
when it goes all over the kitchen floor.

Emma Bradding (8)
Sarisbury CE Junior School

SEASONS

What I like about the spring is
all the tall, yellow flowers growing again,
What I hate about the spring is
it can be very hot.

What I like about summer is
it's hot and sunny,
What I hate about summer is
that it never snows.

What I like about autumn is
when all the brown leaves fall
and I hide underneath them.
What I hate about the autumn is
it's very windy.

What I like about winter is
you can throw white, soft snowballs
at each other.
What I hate about winter is
it's very cold.

Adrian Cross (8)
Sarisbury CE Junior School

LIKES AND HATES

What I like about mummies is
that they make lovely pictures.

What I hate about mummies is
that they smack your bottom
when you're naughty.

What I like about mummies is
when they cheer you up.

What I hate about mummies is
when they tell you what to do.

What I like about mummies is
they are kind and helpful.

Zak Harvey (7)
Sarisbury CE Junior School

LIKES AND HATES

What I like about cats
Is the gentle sound of them purring
What I hate about cats
Is they can be vicious and bite.

What I like about oranges
Is they are juicy and sweet,
What I hate about oranges
Is the pips get in the way.

What I like about art
Is you get to paint.
What I hate about art
Is you get all messy.

What I like about the North Pole
Is you get to play with the snow,
What I hate about the North Pole
Is it is too cold.

What I like about the sun
Is you can play outside,
What I hate about the sun
Is you can get sunburnt.

Lucy Chaplin (7)
Sarisbury CE Junior School

LIKES AND HATES

What I like about tigers
Is their fantastic stripy fur.

What I hate about tigers
Is their sharp claws.

What I like about tigers
Is they can scare annoying adults.

What I hate about tigers
Is they can hurt me quite badly.

What I like about tigers
Is their sharp, shiny, sparkling teeth.

What I hate about tigers
Is they think people are tasty.

What I like about tigers
Is their long furry tail.

What I hate about tigers
Is their angry ferocious face.

What I like about tigers
Is their bright and dark, fantastic colour.

What I hate about tigers
Is they're too big to handle.

Joe Williams (8)
Sarisbury CE Junior School

RIVER POEM

Trickling slowly to form a tiptoeing stream
Flowing lazily along a twisting river
Climbing over weak pebbles
Shallow waters silently creep

Starting to rapidly run, gushing waterfall
Flying dangerously down, smashing upon strong rocks
Dodging determinedly around rough rocks
Rushing towards a great deep sea from a huge mouth.

Emma Dawson (9)
Sarisbury CE Junior School

LIKES AND HATES

What I like about pancakes
is they are hot and you can put jam,
lemon and sugar all over them.

What I hate about pancakes
is they always crumble up when
you leave them too long.

What I like about sweets
is they're delicious and chewy and sticky.

What I hate about sweets
is they always hurt my teeth and I have to
go to the dentist.

What I like about ice cream
is it's cold and tastes good.

What I hate about ice cream
is it gets too hot and melts.

What I like about drinks
is they're cold, refreshing and fizzy.

What I hate about drinks
is when I spill them, I have to clean
them up with kitchen roll.

Tom Cooper (8)
Sarisbury CE Junior School

LIKE AND HATE

What I hate about summer
is the seagulls.

What I like about summer
is it's hot and sunny.

What I hate about summer
is that it never snows.

What I like about summer
is that you can go swimming all day.

What I hate about summer
is that the beach is crowded.

What I like about summer
is that the sun glistens so brightly.

What I hate about summer
is that bees come buzzing in your house.

What I like about summer
is that it's so quiet.

What I hate about summer
is that in the streets it is so busy.

Tristan Rebbettes (7)
Sarisbury CE Junior School

RIVERS

Tiptoeing slyly over weak pebbles
Rivers running rapidly like a raging bull
Sprinting viciously, as fast as an athlete
Twisting and turning around the meander
Creeping, curling, a lazy buzzing bee

Flying over waterfalls, a seagull swooping
Plunging blindly
Lashing clumsily
Gushing uncontrollably to the mouth of the river.
Flowing endlessly.

Vicky Whitcombe (10)
Sarisbury CE Junior School

BEFORE THE BATTLE

Battle allies
comfort me.

Dark brown mud
catch me if I fall.

Big black gun
help me.

Uproar of noise
give me confidence.

As leaves fall from the trees,
I slice my way through the enemy.
As acorns hit the ground,
bullets pound my helmet.

Camouflage,
hide me.

Drops of rain,
clothe my footsteps.

Guiding compass,
steer me home to safety.

Matthew Gordon (8)
Sarisbury CE Junior School

LIKES AND HATES

What I like about TV is
that I can watch all of
my favourite programs.

What I hate about TV is
when I watch it for too long
I get a headache.

What I like about chocolate is
it's tasty and it
melts in my mouth.

What I hate about chocolate is
there are so many different kinds
so that when I want milk chocolate
I end up with plain, and that is horrible!

What I like about the bath is
that it is all bubbly and warm.

What I hate about the bath is
when I get out and the heater
isn't on, so I get all cold.

What I like about walking is
I can see everything without
going really fast.

What I hate about walking is
when I walk for too long,
my legs start to hurt.

Nadine Snoswell (8)
Sarisbury CE Junior School

LIKES AND HATES

What I like about my teacher
is that she's kind and helpful,
What I hate about my teacher
is she makes me do all my work.

What I like about my sister,
is she lets me play with one of her toys.
What I hate about my sister,
is she wakes me up too early in the morning.

What I like about my friends,
is that they care for me,
What I hate about my friends,
is that sometimes when I want to play with them,
they don't want to play with me.

What I like about ice cream,
is that it's tasty to eat,
What I hate about ice cream,
is that it's freezing cold.

What I like about my mummy,
is she helps me when I'm stuck,
What I hate about my mummy
is she nags me.

What I like about my daddy,
is he plays with me,
What I hate about my daddy,
is he shouts at me.

Louise Sykes (7)
Sarisbury CE Junior School

RIVERS

T he River Hamble
H as many meanders
E very one, like a slithery snake

R iver is the name
I 've seen a lot of rivers
V ery cold, some rivers are
E very one as cold as ice
R iver is the name

H eavy rocks turn into stone
A s they flow down the river
M any rivers flow very fast
B ut some go very slow
L ike a snail
E very river has a name.

Thomas Dexter (10)
Sarisbury CE Junior School

SCHOOL

What I hate about school
is doing maths
What I like about school
is doing painting
What I hate about school
is doing assembly
What I like about school
is IET and the library
What I like about school
is the video.

Jessica Harrison (7)
Sarisbury CE Junior School

THE RIVER TEST

T he river meanders
H ot could never be mentioned
E nd of the river is a mouth.

R iver is the name
I t sometimes makes a lake
V ery, very deep is a lake
E verybody has seen a river
R ivers sometimes open into the sea.

T est is a river
E veryone has see it
S ome people live on it
T ributary is where two rivers join.

Joseph Simpson (10)
Sarisbury CE Junior School

THE SLEEPOVER

Chitter chatter, chitter chatter,
Wicked!
Chitter chatter, chitter chatter,
Why not?
Let's make a plan, let's make a plan,
Let's eat, let's eat,
Yum, yum,
Crunch, crunch,
I'm tired,
Yawn, yawn,
Zzzz . . .

Amy Heathorn (9)
Sarisbury CE Junior School

FOOTBALL

What I hate about football
Is getting dirty and muddy
And having a bath
At home after the match.

What I like about football
Is diving and saving goals and diving around
And saving goals and passing and
Shooting and scoring goals.

What I hate about football
Is letting in goals and not scoring
In a match.

What I like about football
If you are the captain of your team
You are in charge of your team.

What I hate about football
Is you have to get up early to play a
Match or training with your team for
One or two hours.

Kyle Graham (8)
Sarisbury CE Junior School

WHAT IS NIGHT?

Night is like a dense forest,
where yellow eyes peer out of the blackness
of the trees.

Night is like a black cavern
where the calls of birds echo
off the rocky walls.

Night is like a dark, oily lake,
where shadows dance across the
surface in silence.

Night is like a black crow,
which flies through the inky darkness
in search of food.

Catriona Parfitt (8)
Sarisbury CE Junior School

SCHOOL

What I hate about school
Is going to assembly
What I like about school
Is going to the Library.
What I hate about school
Is getting told off for writing on the whiteboard.
What I like about school
Is writing on the whiteboard.
What I hate about school
Is doing science.
What I like about school
Is lining up at night to go home
What I hate about school
Is the smell of the dinner hall.
What I like about school
Is going outside to the playground.
What I hate about school
Is staying and finishing work.
What I like about school
Is watching TV.

Sarah Field (8)
Sarisbury CE Junior School

ME AT SCHOOL

What I like about school
Is eating my delicious lunch in our
colourful dinner hall.

What I hate about school
Is the endless math's tests.

What I like about school
Is creating on word art.

What I hate about school
Is when teachers go on and on and on
I get bored!

What I like about school
Is playing 'It' with my friends
at break time.

What I hate about school
Is Assembly time, unless we sing
my favourite song
'Seek ye first'.

What I hate about school
Is doing PE in freezing cold playground.

What I like about school
Is getting messy in art.

Lorna Light (8)
Sarisbury CE Junior School

A RIVER

Glittering water,
Shining in the bright sunlight,
Shimmering shadows.

Swishing and splashing,
Raging, bashing on the bank,
Slushy surfaces.

Crumbling damp bank,
Tumbling, making a gorge,
Rippling waters.

Rapids rushing down,
Tumbling, crashing pebbles,
Making a flood plain.

Crystal clear blue skies,
Sunlight raging down on me,
Feeling very hot.

Dangerously beating,
Flowing down the river bend,
Crackly, tapping.

Meanders, curving,
Trickling bubbles of fish,
Foaming waterfall.

Annabel Sims (9)
Sarisbury CE Junior School

DOGS

What I hate about dogs
Is when they slobber over you, putting disgusting, wet
Dribble on you by licking.
What I like about dogs
Is their delicate, soft fur in different colours.
What I like about dogs,
Is their playful personality and their cuddly
Body as well.
What I hate about dogs
Is when they step on your feet, it hurts!
What I like about dogs
Is their beautiful, staring eyes.
What I hate about dogs
Is when they give you a painful bite.
What I like about dogs
Is their big legs that run really fast.

Katie Porter (8)
Sarisbury CE Junior School

THE RIVER

T empting water patters tingly on the muddy ground
H eaving down the sharp pointed mountain
E ndless steps the river rushes

R apidly running the meandering turns
I nterrupted by the steep plunging steps of waterfalls
V iciously crashes against the blunt rocks
E dging slowly, freedom awaits
R ushes past the tributary sea is arriving.

Ashley York (10)
Sarisbury CE Junior School

HEDGEHOGS

What I like about hedgehogs
Is their cute little feet which scuffle
along the ground.

What I hate about hedgehogs
Is they make a lot of noise in hedges.

What I like about hedgehogs
Is you can trip over them in the night.

What I hate about hedgehogs
Is their tiny little beady-eyes when they
stare at me and I stare back.

What I hate about hedgehogs
is they eat everything.

Jordan Sevier (8)
Sarisbury CE Junior School

THE JOURNEY

Trickling cautiously over the tiny pebbles
Gradually flowing into a slithering stream
Suddenly diving dangerously
To the deep dark depths of a dreaded pool
Dashing and lashing
Whilst spinning and swirling
Slowly edging towards real rapids
Determinedly bashing aimlessly
Before the frantic powerful endless river
Meets the surging sea.

Will Self (10)
Sarisbury CE Junior School

DOGS

What I hate about dogs
Is when they bite you with long sharp teeth.

What I like about dogs
Is when a tiny puppy gives me a cuddle.

What I hate about dogs
Is when they scratch me on the back of my hand.

What I like about dogs
Is giving them a chocolate drop.

What I hate about dogs
Is their slimy wet tongues on you.

What I hate about dogs
Is when they ruin our stuff at home.

What I like about dogs
Is when they kiss me.

What I hate about dogs
Is when they lick me all over my body.

What I like about dogs
Is when I come home and they jump up on me.

What I hate about dogs
Is when they rip our curtains.

What I like about dogs
Is when they have puppies.

Laura Harman (8)
Sarisbury CE Junior School

THE ROUTINE OF A RIVER

Twisting and turning down a dip
As the source is now prepared,
The raindrops are gathering
While the little ones are scared.

Splashing, bending carelessly
Down the alley of clear pebbles
As it turns, now the sound erupts,
Like a group of screaming trebles.

Racing and tumbling around the corner
Now the step is clear
They all plunge off
Flowing, full of no fear.

Rushing and crashing
Tempted to overflow
Spreading across the wide space
Each droplet on the go.

Following, joining,
Two streams ready to bind
Dawdling lazily
Like they had their own mind.

Dancing and tiptoeing
Until they reach their dream,
Here is the mouth of the sea,
It's as cold as ice cream.

Maria Colmer (10)
Sarisbury CE Junior School

I Am A River

I am a river
Upon a high hill,
I'm only small
I keep quite still.

I join other rivers
Who make me stronger,
They take me down
And make me longer.

Then I reach
A rocky wall,
I wash it down
To make a waterfall.

Next I meander
Round and round,
Swaying and bending
Without a sound.

Then I come
To a dip in the ground,
And form a lake
Making lots of sound.

Then I finally
Reach the sea,
And that is how
You now know me.

And now you know
The cycle of a river,
And how I come
And go in the weather.

And how I started
Upon the hill,
Where I stood
Silent and still.

Samantha Whitehead (10)
Sarisbury CE Junior School

SCHOOL

What I hate about school
Is playing in the playground on
cold, winter days.

What I like about school
Is going into the dinner hall and
smelling the delicious dinners.

What I hate about school
Is when teachers talk to one another.

What I like about school
Is going on the computer and
finding out information.

What I hate about school
Is doing loads of maths.

What I like about school
Is doing literacy and especially
doing poetry writing.

Katie Bradding (8)
Sarisbury CE Junior School

RIVERS

A meander of a river is when it curls
But it's scared all the people off like a snake
And it slides like a slithery snake
The wicked waves crash against the rocks
As the meander starts to move
Down the hill
Over it goes, to make a lake
Until it goes over
And joins another source.
It goes off the edge to make a waterfall
Then meanders until it goes into a flood
The flood goes into the mouth
And now you know all about
Rivers.

Matthew Eyres (9)
Sarisbury CE Junior School

DEADLY DEEPS

Rushing, gushing, dashing, lushing
Turning, twisting, plunging viciously
Into deadly deeps of the waterfall.

Swerving, swirling, slyly diving
Dangerously past the unbreakable rocks
Water endlessly deep and mighty
Under bridge, dark and scary.

Under the water sparkling clean fish, all colours by the sea
Waves are tumbling powerfully breaking
A shark full of energy normally, is weak and waiting.

Lauren Lyons-Davis (10)
Sarisbury CE Junior School

WATERFALL

Gushing to the mountain, forming
    a powerful waterfall,
      falling and making a
    Sprayful shower, flowing
with all its mighty power over
    the pebbles and rocks.
      Flowing, falling, trying to get
    away for the powerful
   water trickling over the edge
  of the whinstone, blowing, bugging
trying to get through, falling
  ferociously, splattering everywhere, gushing,
    the water is a raging rapid
      crawling slowly, calming down now.

Emily Clarke (9)
Sarisbury CE Junior School

THE JOURNEY

A creeping sound the river makes as it blindly starts to form,
Trickling over the slippery pebbles
Slithering between them, like a determined snake.
Turning into a tiptoeing stream, silently towing along,
Gradually widening the river edges towards a sudden drop,
Plunging down the steep waterfall.
Suddenly smashing into vicious steel rocks,
Trying to lap over them,
Fighting determinedly until the river is free.
Striding along, fully formed, turning twisted, sharp turns,
Until it reaches the widening mouth,
Slowly creeps into the deadly polluted sea.

Caitlan Burch (10)
Sarisbury CE Junior School

WHAT AM I?

I'm a flowing body of liquid
I trickle down steep hills, I sparkle!
I'm crystal clear!
I sound like the quiet whisper of children,
I glisten in the sparkling sun,
I silently drift slowly,
Oh no!
Getting bigger, turning into rapids.
I'm now bubbly, no longer slow,
No longer silent, now I'm rushing,
Racing dangerously.

What am I?

Frankie Fullick (10)
Sarisbury CE Junior School

WHAT I HATE AND LIKE ABOUT TIGERS

I hate the way that tigers walk so slowly
they scare people as well.

I like it when they roar and show
their sharp teeth.

I hate it when they run for their prey.

I like tigers when they are soft and warm
and their habitat is so African and blue.

So come on tigers, we can make it better for you.

Emily Mills (8)
Sarisbury CE Junior School

WHAT IS IT?

It rushes down on to rocks
It's a slithery snake,
It forms a lake
It is as strong as a lion.
It has a mind of its own
It has not a single bone,
It runs away
It goes into the sea.
Is as green as a pea
It meets up with others
It starts on a mountain,
Sometimes it's a water fountain.
It's all water
It splashes on rocks,
It does not care who it knocks
It will never run out.
What is it?

Hannah Goff (9)
Sarisbury CE Junior School

THE RIVER

Tumbling and gushing the waterfall crashed
Clashing against the steel rocks
Flowing deeply, flooding a landing
As the sprinting river shoots down the lake.

Swerving and twisting round tight bends
Racing powerfully towards the waterfall
Lashing against the rocky, crumbly sides of the river.

Daniel Butler (9)
Sarisbury CE Junior School

Before The Battle

Squelching mud
Support me
Gigantic trees
Hide me
Furious guns
Protect me
Camouflage
Protect my
Every move I make
I run to safety
People ran
Quickly as
Machine guns fire
Helmets protect my head
Lead me to my fight.

Zakk Raby (9)
Sarisbury CE Junior School

The Waterfall

W aterfall comes down like a bird
A   small stream comes from the waterfall
T   iny deep lakes form
E   xcellent river dives for another waterfall
R   iver comes from the waterfall again
F   alling waterfall stays for days
A   nd goes down to the sea
L   ake carries on and on
L   eaves drop from trees and drown in the waterfall.

Natasha Davey (9)
Sarisbury CE Junior School

MY BIG DOG

What I hate about my big dog is
she steps on my toes with her big feet.
What I like about my big dog is
she has soft grey and white fur.
What I hate about my big dog is
she gets awfully muddy then she shakes very hard.
What I like about my big dog is
she can eat things off the table.
What I hate about my big dog is
she bites my face but not very hard.
What I like about my big dog is
she falls asleep very quickly.
What I hate about my big dog is
she barks in the morning and wakes me up.
What I like about my big dog is
she licks my face with her strong tongue.

Andrew Dore (8)
Sarisbury CE Junior School

THE WATERFALL

W   ater plunging over steep dynamic rocks
A   lmighty roars as it dives actively
T   rickling water hazardously crashes
E   normous waves plunge, polishing stones
R   apidly crashing like a violent bull
F   rothy bubbles form the river bath
A   ggressively like a lion
L   azy water wanders off
L   aunching itself in the lonesome sea.

Kim Gannaway (10)
Sarisbury CE Junior School

WHAT I LIKE AND WHAT I HATE

What I hate about rain
Is you have to wear a coat.

What I hate about rain
Is it falls on your head and makes your hair wet.

What I hate about rain
Is when you have no umbrella you get drenched.

What I hate about rain
Is it's so wet you get your hair wet.

What I like about rain
Is when you are hot it cools you down.

What I like about rain
Is that is makes puddles to splash in.

What I like about rain
Is you can splash in it.

Grace Nash (8)
Sarisbury CE Junior School

WHAT'S THAT?

What's that I hear behind me?
It's screeching and it's snappy
By the creaking of the floor
And the opening of your door
Oh, you know it's out there somewhere.

What's that I hear behind me?
It sounds pretty slimy
I don't want to know
I just want it to go
Leave me alone!

What's that I hear behind me?
I've had it now, I've got to see
Round went my head
Across the soft edge of my bed
Oh, I know it's out there somewhere.

Charlotte Burgess (9)
Sarisbury CE Junior School

THE LIFE OF A RIVER

Rainfall, rainfall coming down
Source of a river is starting
Down the hill rushing around
Crashing down from the top of a waterfall
And shimmers on.

Sharply, swiftly
Turning and twisting
Down huge rapids.

Slowing down now
And turning around a great meander
And crashing into the edge.

Going incredibly slowly down
And dropping dirt to make a flood plain.

Rushing in and out of islands
Trying to get to the mouth
Dodging rocks and scraping the floor and edge.

Entered mouth now and racing into the sea
And leaping with joy like a little boy
For the end of a river's life.

Joshua Braybrooke (10)
Sarisbury CE Junior School

My Sister

What I hate about my sister
Is that she talks in her sleep and is so annoying.

What I like about my sister
Is that sometimes she plays with me, so it makes
me feel happy.

What I hate about my sister
Is that she barges into my room without knocking
on the door.

What I like about my sister
Is that sometimes she goes to her friend's house
so I can have time to myself.

What I hate about my sister
Is she hurts me sometimes and it hurts.

What I like about my sister
Is that she lets me use her Game Boy.

Katie Hartland (8)
Sarisbury CE Junior School

River System

Tiptoeing gracefully down the alley of rocks
Flowing rapidly to the waterfall
Dashing so determinedly
With no fears at all.

Stumbling furiously down the empty gap
Smashing on the jagged rocks
Diving and darting lively
Like a hungry hunting fox.

Meandering drowsily, creeping to the end
Swooping slyly to the open sea
Coming to the delta and mouth
Rushing eagerly.

Crushing to the meeting of the sea
River and sea mixing gleefully
Constantly from the source
To get to the end repetitively.

Stephanie Churcher (9)
Sarisbury CE Junior School

SOMETHING IN MY BEDROOM

There's something in my bedroom
Oh, I don't really care
Suddenly it comes a rattling just over there
It sounds like the rattle of the biscuits in the tin
But nobody's downstairs, I must be dreaming.

There's something in my bedroom
Something I cannot see
My sister is snoring loud and fast
Why did this happen to me?
I always feel scared after I go to bed
'Just go to sleep,' is what my mother said.

There's something in my bedroom
I felt like this yesterday
My heart is beating fast
I want it to go away
I am sure that there is something
It's just I don't know where!

Fleur Spencer (8)
Sarisbury CE Junior School

THE RIVER

Gushing waterfalls
Race rapidly down the streams
Crashing against sharp rocks
Through the clear water that gleams.

> Rough, rushing rapids
> Rumble, roar down the river
> Foaming water swirls
> Makes the animals quiver.

Pike hunt, Minnows pray
Suddenly a sparkling splash
Minnows swim quickly
There's a sudden silence.

> *Crash*!

Chloe Nicholson (10)
Sarisbury CE Junior School

THE RIVER

Out from the source, gushes crystal clear
A glistening trickle of water,
Down it flows over big rocky boulders near
Banks of purple prickly heather.

Water from rain washed hills
Forms tributaries joining the slowly growing stream
The river plunging over a granite rock sill
Falling gracefully creating a beautiful rainbow dream.

Crashing viciously while twisting and turning around
Teetering on the edge before lashing on the rocks
Flows overboard until reaching the ground
Then they all sprint on their blue frocks.

The river widens and deepens
Meandering lazily through glades and patchwork
Meadows filled with flowers.
The rippling river separates and opens
Through the estuaries meeting the sea.

Lucy Garner (9)
Sarisbury CE Junior School

RIVER HAIKU

Rivers start at source
And finishes at the mouth
Twirling down rapids.

         Rushing waterfalls
         Pouring shiny waters roar
         Like a huge lion.

Plunge pools racing fast
Swirling, rushing all around
Crashing heavily.

         Swirling and whirling
         Glides through windy meanders
         Gushing and rushing.

Lauren Klinkosz (10)
Sarisbury CE Junior School

MY ADVENTURE

Rushing waters
Raging rapids
Crashing waterfalls
Ruining rocks
Foaming fountains
Sparkling streams
Gigantic gorges
Dropping valleys
Bending rivers.

Fish are sleeping, sun is shining
The sun is beaming, burning brightly
Strolling, slowing, sparkling downwards
The bubbling roar of me
The grit tickles me as the weeds wrap my legs
I get older, I need to drop off sediment
I am here all that way for nothing, is this my end?

Daniel Harris (9)
Sarisbury CE Junior School

IN THE GRAVEYARD

When I was in bed one night
All tucked up tight
A noise from the graveyard
Made me sit upright.

I crept out of my bed
All those noises in my head
Peeling back the curtains
There's nothing there I'm certain.

I open up the window
The wind blows back my hair
I check outside again
But still there's nothing there.

The noise outside has stopped now
By the feel so has my heart
I go and turn on the light
And all of a sudden it's not so dark.

Hannah Lothian (8)
Sarisbury CE Junior School

THE RIVER'S LIFE

Rapids rapidly rush,
Down the mountain flush,
Really small, really quick,
Over falls does it flick,
Crystal clear, getting near; near to the sea!

Getting slower, getting older,
Bashing at a hard boulder,
Swirling, curling, whirling round,
Flooding slowly on the ground,
Crystal clear, getting nearer; nearer to the sea!

There was once a river,
Getting old and withered,
Really big and really slow,
Near the sea does it go,
Crystal clear, getting close; now it's at the end!

Samuel Derham (10)
Sarisbury CE Junior School

MY SISTER

What I like about my sister is
she always gives me lots of hugs.
What I hate about my sister is
when she has a fight with me.
What I like about my sister is
she gives me gingerbread men on her birthday
What I hate about my sister is
she has the light on when she can't sleep
What I like about my sister is
when I am unhappy she leaves me alone if I want her to
What I hate about my sister is
when I hurt myself she laughs at me.
What I like about my sister is
when we are on holiday she is really kind to me.
What I hate about my sister is
I have to share a room with her.
What I like about my sister is
she laughs at the jokes I say.
What I hate about my sister is
she nicks my stuff without asking.
What I like about my sister is
when we get along with each other.
What I hate about my sister is
most of the time she is mean to me.

Zoë Whitcombe (8)
Sarisbury CE Junior School

A River's Journey

A stream
trickles and tiptoes down rock
like a young thin boy
into a gorge
Rushing and rumbling
the deep dark sides
Glides into rapids
punching rocks and crashing banks in anger
A swooping waterfall
drags it down to its plunge pool
where it splashes out of control
a calm meander
gently swoops it round its twisting bends
Finally in the sea
now it relaxes and can flow anywhere
greeting new rivers.

Martin Lander (10)
Sarisbury CE Junior School

Raging Rapids

Raging rapids
Beat the rocks
Swiftly scrapes the serrated rocks below
Climbing cliffs, rocking boats
Roaring rapidly past the Pike.

Sam Williams (10)
Sarisbury CE Junior School

THE DOG POEM

What I like about dogs is their soft, smooth fur.
What I hate about dogs is their slobbery, slimy tongue.
What I like about dogs is their feet when they go in the mud
and come in the house putting paw prints on the floor.
What I hate about dogs is when they go into the sea
and get wet, then shake it all over me.

Isobel Hector (7)
Sarisbury CE Junior School

HAPPINESS

Happiness is yellow like the sun shining on the grass,
It tastes like chocolate melting in my mouth.
It smells like Mum's perfume flowing up my nose,
It looks like the bright blue sky going round the world.
It sounds like the wind calmly wafting through the air,
It feels like a bunny rabbit, soft, sweet and beautiful.

Emily Taylor (8)
Townhill Junior School

HAPPINESS

Happiness is bright green like winning the FA Cup.
It tastes like strong mints,
It smells like freshly cut grass.
It looks like waves crashing against the rocks,
It sounds like you're listening into a seashell
It feels like magic.

Mitchell Tongs (9)
Townhill Junior School

MY PET REINDEER

Once a reindeer came to my house
He did my homework, he cleaned my room
And took down the washing,
But the one thing he doesn't do
Is put me to bed.
I do that myself, because he doesn't
Know how to.

Kierran Eldridge (8)
Townhill Junior School

THERE'S SOME JELLY IN MY TUMMY

There's some jelly in my tummy
There's some jelly in my tummy,
And it won't stop wiggling about.
My mum says
'Stop jiggling on the couch!'

James Whitby (8)
Townhill Junior School

HAPPINESS

White, blue, like a summer day
It tastes like a cherry in my mouth,
It smells like fresh spring flowers.
It looks like the sun, bright and shiny,
Sounds like the sea, splashing on the beach.
Feels like soft, fluffy cotton on your skin.

Benjamin Kevin Fox (9)
Townhill Junior School

I'M SCARED

The sky grows orange like fire
That rumbling sound is quite dire,
I hope this house has nothing scary in it.
But then . . .
A bony hand taps every minute
A noise!
A sudden creak upon the stair.
I hope and pray there's nothing there . . .

My heart stops and misses a beat
I can hear it on the landing, coming to eat . . .
'Please God, you are so wow,
you're the only one to save me now
from this terrible *horror!*'

Oh, I do want to get rid of my fear
because this terrible creature is drawing near,

A knock on the door
I feel I'll faint upon the floor

I'm hiding under the eiderdown
I do so wish, I wasn't such a clown
Suddenly
A dazzling light
Brightening up the darkness of the night.

'Go away!'
'Oh Jack, don't be scared, it's only me.'
'Mum?'
'You should be asleep by now.'
Mum tucked me in, and emptied the bin
and went . . .
I'm scared!

Laura Dawkins (9)
Townhill Junior School

WHEN I SANK

I am a swordfish
I am ready to attack!
But something struck
I was gone in a minute
Bugs under the sea eaten
Half of me
And 1982
People lifted
Me up to the surface, they
Put me in a glass frame
Then
I was famous . . .
People
Spraying me
It feels like
I'm being attacked.

Lewis Smith (9)
Townhill Junior School

MY FAMILY

My mum bosses me around
And throws me around,
My brother tosses me around
And annoys me!
I miss my dad,
Because I like him.
But I like my family
I like it as we are.

Jack Kazi (7)
Townhill Junior School

HOW THE MARY ROSE REALLY SUNK

This is the story of the ghost of old,
With her evil eyes aflame,
The ship's the best and the sailors bold,
But that's not really her name.

Her name is Black and she is scary,
The Mary, she didn't have a chance,
The sailors fought and were very weary,
Her lethal poisonous glance.

It was a glance, oh yes, that's all,
That killed the crew right then.
Her magic powers inside her eyeball,
She haunted one of the men.

That man, he caused the death of so many,
And he knew within,
He acted as if he hadn't hurt any,
The ghost was Anne Boleyn.

So Henry the Eighth, his heart was weakening,
But this was just a warning.
The Mary Rose was no longer sinking,
His problems were only dawning.

Now this was how the Mary Rose sunk,
But how King Henry died,
The truth is that he never did,
The archaeologists' lied.

Thomas Diffey (10)
Townhill Junior School

ALPHABET POEM

A is for Alison, who had some clips
B is for Barry, who had some chips,
C is for Cara, who likes the night
D is for Danny, who has a good sight.
E is for Emma, who goes to bed,
F is for Fred, who likes to say 'Said!'
G is for Gemma, who hides in a box,
H is for Harry, who has smelly socks,
I is for Isabel who likes honey,
J is for Joe who has some money.
K is for Katie, who likes to dig holes,
L is for Lucy, who likes her dolls.
M is for Mel, who is always glad
N is for Nick, who is always sad.
O is for Oliver, who has a hat
P is for Pooja, who has a cat
Q is for Queeny, who has a hat,
R is for Rachel, who has a book
S is for Sarah, who has to climb trees
T is for Tim, who likes to eat pies
U is for Ursula who writes a poem
V is for Violet, who has a hen
W is for Wendy, who has a pencil
X is for Xman, who has a stencil.
Y is for Yasmin, who ate a pear,
Z if for Zoe, who has long hair.

Katie Blankley (9)
Townhill Junior School

BEING BULLIED

I hate being bullied
by Jack Jeeves.
Please don't dunk my head in the dirt
or take away my friend.
You're so mean, Jack Jeeves . . .
fighting me like that,
don't get people to join in.
You're so nasty Jack Jeeves . . .
Who do you think you are?
Please don't call me names,
or make me jump,
You're so horrible Jack Jeeves . . .
Why can't you bully someone your own size?
Can you take your hands off me?
Please don't bully me,
Please,
Please,
Don't bully me.

Toby Way (10)
Townhill Junior School

THE MATCH

The commentator spitting into the microphone,
The ball racing to the goal,
The supporters shouting at the team,
The goalkeeper screaming at his players,
The sub's waiting, happy to get on,
The manager yelling at the ref,
The clock is counting up to 90 minutes
The game is over!

Joe Hopkins (10)
Townhill Junior School

FEELINGS

F   eelings make some people feel sad, but not me, I feel glad

E   veryone has feelings, feelings that are sad, some feelings
make you mad
E   ach living being has feelings, sad feelings, happy feelings
some that make you mad.
L   ovely feelings, happy feelings, some that make you cry.

I   have feelings which make me shiver, like I am in a freezing river

N   early every feeling I have, is happy or sad, some about my friends
some about my family.
G   irls have feelings, boy have feelings, animals have feelings too.

S   ome feelings make you worry, some people hurt your feelings,
some you have to keep to yourself.

Jade McLean (7)
Townhill Junior School

THE AMAZING INVISIBLE CAT

First the cat started off as a bat,
It felt strange and poorly,
Then it got fat and lazy
It grew long and fat legs,
It grew a big pair of ears,
Then it was a cat.
Then it went all silver, it was invisible
It got into mischief
And spoiled things up,
And carried on forever.

Jamie Johnson (8)
Townhill Junior School

SNAKES

Snakes silently sliver upon
the grass
Like a poisoned river
flowing past
Sensibly overpowering its prey
with a slimy trail, hissing away.

Snakes shed their skin
for a new plate of armour,
Creeping all day
Sizing up each other.

Snakes' sensors show them the way
Flexing on the trees at night
So you see snakes kill in the jungle
After a day's work, they find a burrow.

Christopher Matthew Garner (11)
Townhill Junior School

HAPPINESS

It tastes as good as chocolate, melting
in my mouth.
It smells as perfumed as a rose.
It looks as shiny as money,
It sounds like a flute playing
soft music.
It feels like someone
doing a good turn.
It's as white as a fluffy cloud
floating in the sky.

Rebecca Harley (9)
Townhill Junior School

MY FAMILY

Sisters, aren't they funny?
Mine goes around
And says she has a bad tummy!

Mums, aren't they tidy?
Mine goes around polishing
'Til the floor is all slidy!

Dads, aren't they lazy?
Mine watches football all day
And is very crazy!

Brothers, aren't they rough?
Mine goes around
And acts so tough!

And me . . .
Well, *I'm perfect!*

Hannah Shaw (11)
Townhill Junior School

SNOW

As white as a dove, flying over the houses,
As cold as a freezer when it is shut.
The thing which children like most,
The thing which parents can't stand.
It falls peacefully from the sky
And lands softly on the ground.
The thing which parents cannot stand
The thing which children love.

Nicola Cooke (11)
Townhill Junior School

MY FRONT ROOM'S A MESS!

My front room's a mess
It looks like the lake of Loch Ness
A lake of books
But no fish hooks.
We have a monster
Who's my little brother.
He looks like a monster thing
From somewhere or other.
Even though my front room's a mess
Hopefully next week,
There will be a little bit less.

Thomas O'Meara (11)
Townhill Junior School

BLUEBELLS

The calling wind spirals through the trees,
Greeting the ringing bells.

Mini light bulbs sprout tiny turquoise shoots,
Climbing towards the glowing sun.

Heads of silver blue, defend their tender roots,
The river of blue flows freely
through the open space.

When the golden sun appears,
Your bell-like heads, great local walkers with a smile.

Joanna Woolley (11)
Townhill Junior School

DESERT

The desert is full
of hot, soft sand,
Dangerous, blinding sand . . .
It is a home
A massive home for animals,
Desert rats, lizards
and beetles.

When the sand swirls
and blows
I cover my face
and sit down
To let the storm pass.
When it has passed
I drink avidly from my water bottle,
Quenching my thirst.
Then I carry on towards home.

Rebecca Penfold (11)
Townhill Junior School

ANGER

My anger is as red as blood,
It tastes like a sour lemon,
It smells like the salty sea.
It looks like a volcano erupting,
It sounds like a driller drilling,
It feels like fire burning.

Jordan Doling (9)
Townhill Junior School

TAKING ADVICE

I got beaten up today
It wasn't very nice
I went home to see my dad
And get some advice

He told me to fight back
Retaliate if you can
Show him who's boss
He's messing with my Sam

I wasn't sure if he was right
So I went to Mum
I told her my problem
She said 'Go get my gun'

I got home from school today
Mum and Dad weren't very nice
All because I had taken
Their very silly advice.

Sam Collins (10)
Townhill Junior School

MY SADNESS

My sadness is blue like the dark starry night,
And it tastes like the salty seawater from the ocean.
The smells it makes are like the bark from an old dead tree,
It looks like rotten leaves, scurrying along the grass,
The sound it makes is like a car crash.
That's what sadness is to me.

Laura Noyce (9)
Townhill Junior School

THE MAGIC RUBBER

One day I found a rubber
On the bathroom floor,
And you would never guess what,
But . . . I erased the bathroom door.

When I got to class that day
I erased the entire school
I was feeling so great because
My friends thought it was cool

When it got to playtime
I had some time to spend
And I was busy playing 'tab'
But I accidentally rubbed out my friend.

And at the end of the day
I didn't know what to do
I had my rubber confiscated
And I was glad of that too.

Danielle Clements (10)
Townhill Junior School

MY HAPPINESS

My happiness is as orange as the sun on a blazing hot day
It tastes like melting chocolate in your mouth,
And smells like cola, looks like ice cream.
Sounds like orange juice pouring into the cup,
It feels like soft pillows against your cheeks.
That's all my happiness.

Philippa Alford (9)
Townhill Junior School

MY HAPPINESS

My happiness is pink,
It looks like bubbling candyfloss.
My happiness tastes like pink apple pie,
The smell of my happiness is like fresh flowers.
It sounds like birds chirping in the morning,
The feeling of happiness is a soft teddy bear.
That is my happiness in life.

Kate Louise Hughes (9)
Townhill Junior School

HAPPINESS

Happiness is going on holiday to Australia to see sharks under glass
Happiness is dancing in the moonlight
Happiness is to go into space to see the moon
Happiness is doing gymnastics
Happiness is seeing your mum on television
Happiness is to teach a baby to walk
Happiness is to see a castle.

Jordan Panella (9)
Townhill Junior School

HAPPINESS

A huge smiley face waiting for a cuddle
Friends all whispering in a huddle.
Tastes like cream in a bundle,
It looks like yellow for a smiley face,
It feels like an outing to a lovely place
Happiness is a fantasy in an expressioned face.

Chloe Harris (9)
Townhill Junior School

GRANDAD'S DOG

Tilly is a silly dog
She runs around all day
And every time I see her
We just play, play and play!

James Hollick (8)
Townhill Junior School

LIST POEMS

Blue is a dolphin, swimming through the ocean free
Blue is the sky with clouds wafting through the blue sky
Blue is a river splashing across the country
Blue is the rain tipping down buckets of water, making puddles
Blue is the world covered by sea
Blue is a road sign, giving instructions to keep you safe
Blue is most people's favourite colour, most of the time
Blue is the colour of a horrible homework folder
Blue is the colour of my amazing art diary

Staci Clark (9)
Townhill Junior School

SILLY OLD DOG

Silly old dog, fell in the bog
Went to the loo, fell down it too,
Fell down the stair, landed on his bear,
Where's that pet? He's at the vet!

David Fotheringham (7)
Townhill Junior School

THE BEE

I went outside to look at the tree,
Suddenly a bee flew into me.
The bee stung me all over the place,
It stung me, especially on my face.

Pooja Rajguru (10)
Townhill Junior School

CONTRAST

A cold face
Hard as stone
Cruel heart
Falling
Falling

A warm face
Comforting
A smile
A hug
I feel better

David Williams (11)
Townhill Junior School

WHAT I THOUGHT

I used to think paramedics were only men,
I used to think teachers were only women.
I used to think my brother was annoying,
Until I annoyed him.

Matthew Day (8)
Townhill Junior School

THE SUN

A red bright shiny sun
It tastes like crisp burnt toast
Smells like ashes from the hot fire
It looks like flaming bubbly lava
Sounds like the munching of raspberries
Feels like smooth flames.

Sophie O'Donnell (8)
Townhill Junior School

BROTHERS

I like to annoy my brother
And get him into lots of bother,
When he plays football
I trip him up and make him fall.
He chases me up the road,
I run away and shout 'You ugly old toad!'
Then my mum calls us in for tea
And I'm as nice as I can be.

Rosanna Lane (7)
Townhill Junior School

FEAR

My fear is as black as the night sky,
It tastes of sour curry on a gloomy night.
It smells of cloudy smoke from a burning fire,
It looks like a quiet person in their grave.
It sounds like a screaming child about to die,
It feels like a vampire making you cry.

Laura-Jane Robson (9)
Townhill Junior School

There's A Monster In My Room

There's a monster under my bed
And it's swallowed Mum and Dad
I think there's a caveman in my wardrobe
And he leaves his bones under my pillow
There's a goblin on my roof
It eats cats and dogs.
There's fur in the fireplace
I shout . . .
'Help! Help!'

Alex Hart (8)
Townhill Junior School

Snakes

Snakes slither in the grass
Hard to see as we walk past
Just be careful where you tread
A poisonous snake, we all dread
Lying in the summer sun
Snakes warm up to have some fun.

Kieran Oliphant (8)
Townhill Junior School

All About My Teeth

Drilling and filling
Munching and crunching
Injections and inspections
Chomping and chewing

Tugging and plugging
Sucking and slurping
Fixing and mixing
I wish I'd brushed and flossed.

Suzanne Gavagan (8)
Townhill Junior School

LITTLE MISS DAISY

Little Miss Daisy
Loved to be lazy
Staying in bed all day
Her mother got mad
And said she was bad
And took all her bedclothes away.

Rebecca Quilter (8)
Townhill Junior School

MY POEM

F   ootball is my favourite sport,
O   n Friday's and Saturday's I go training.
O   n Sunday's we play matches
T   hough it could be raining.
B   ut even if it's wet or the ball is in our net
A   s long as you enjoy it,
L   ook up and don't be glum,
L   ose, win or draw, it's all fun.

Bradley Snelling (7)
Townhill Junior School

THE JUNGLE ROOM

My room
Is a jungle

The swinging vines of socks
Creeping around the room
Along with the scary tigers
Underneath my bed

The towering tree
Covering my desk
With a terrible hissing snake
Crawling along the leaves

When I look out my windows
I see all the wildlife
I pretend that the badgers
Are creeping, crawling cheetahs

My room
Is a jungle
Full of sad
And happy memories.

Jake Willis (10)
Townhill Junior School

WRITING POEMS

I have a poem to write
It's going to take all night
I don't know what to call it
I'd rather write a story.

Max Trayhorn (8)
Townhill Junior School

My Garden Bugs

As I stroll through my garden,
There're lots of insects and bugs,
Like ants, beetles and ladybirds,
Worms, snails and slugs.

They creep along the patio,
Fly swiftly through the trees,
Climb up the old brick wall,
Hop through the grass so green.

If I were to choose,
My favourite of them all,
Are butterflies and ladybirds,
Which are colourful, not dull.

Hannah Aston (11)
Townhill Junior School

Guinea Pigs

G   uinea pigs are my favourite animals
U   nderneath the hay they sleep
I   love to see them scamper about
N   ervous little creatures they are
E   ating is their favourite pastime
A   t night, they snuggle up to sleep

P   lenty of cuddles I give them when they're cold
I   love them very much
G   uinea pigs make perfect pets
S   o go and buy one now.

Rianna Leonard (8)
Townhill Junior School

WHITE LAND

I'm up in the white land,
Such a picturesque place,
Where lochs glisten like tears.
I go past the frosty soft snow and see
Icicles sparkling, shiny
Thousands of deer and stags, staring and
Gleaming at us, running in groups.
Slipping and sliding across the ice.
The mountain is a cone, upside down with
Vanilla ice cream, thick and deep.
The lochs are puddles of blueberry sauce.
The deer and stags are little sprinkles
Scattered everywhere.

Alex Mark Hibberd (11)
Townhill Junior School

THE MARY ROSE . . . GONE!

I am a shark
Ready to strike my prey
I cannot see them,
But I know they are there.
Crash!
Something has hit me,
But I don't know what.
I have tipped like a cradle,
My friends have left me
I am gone.

Joel Tyrie (10)
Townhill Junior School

DOING . . .

Doing

Digging

Jumping

Diving

Driving

Swimming

Surviving

Is best

Joshua Sheppard (8)
Townhill Junior School

SPACE

Saturn is a doughnut
The moon is a cauliflower
The galaxy is thousands of raisins
Earth is a mixture of blueberry and mint
Moron Mountain is an Easter egg
Spaceships are ice creams
Mars is a Mars bar
Jupiter is whipped cream
Pluto is a cube of ice
My world is a flower
The gravity is wind

Space itself is a big, black carpet.

Sarah Chun (8)
Townhill Junior School